T0128324

IF THE WORLD EXISTS, THEN GOD EXISTS

Argument, Evidence, and Applications

by

JOHN T. WINTHROP

IF THE WORLD EXISTS, THEN GOD EXISTS
ARGUMENT, EVIDENCE, AND APPLICATIONS

iUniverse books may be ordered through booksellers or by contacting:

iUniverse
1663 Liberty Drive
Bloomington, IN 47403
www.iuniverse.com
844-349-9409

ISBN: 978-1-6632-0190-4 (sc)
ISBN: 978-1-6632-0189-8 (e)

Library of Congress Control Number: 2020913349

Print information available on the last page.

iUniverse rev. date: 12/21/2020

For Riga, Greg and Maria

Contents

Preface

This is the second of two books dealing with the structure of reality. In the first of these[1] I claim to solve by system-theoretic means the *problem of the external world*, demonstrating beyond a reasonable doubt the reality of an external world of space-time, matter and energy. In the present volume I claim to solve in a related way the *problem of God*, demonstrating beyond a reasonable doubt the existence of the three-in-one God of monotheism. Both arguments proceed from the Principle named in the first book's title, and both are empirically testable.

The Principle of True Representation (PTR) [1] is a metaphysical principle, asserting that to exist is to be truthfully self-representing. Thus the two books considered together entail the interaction of three distinct disciplines: theology (God), metaphysics (the PTR), and physics (space-time, matter and energy). Picture a triangle whose vertices represent the three disciplines and the sides their interaction, as depicted in figure (a) below. We see that the first book relates to side 1 of the triangle (interaction between physics and metaphysics), and the present one to side 2 (interaction between theology and metaphysics). But, crucially, the present book entails side 3 as well (interaction between theology and physics). For in this book we show the logical structure of God to be isomorphic to that of the physical world, implying—indeed, necessitating— the presence of a transcendent source of the world's lawful structure, namely, God. That in a nutshell is what I am calling the *existential argument* for the existence of God, a formal demonstration at once justifying monotheism and falsifying atheism.

This is not the first time that theology, metaphysics, and physics have figured collectively in a theory of knowledge. More than a century after the publication of Newton's *Principia* (1687) and the advent of scientific method, Auguste Comte (1798-1857) claimed that one could track the evolution of Western intellectual development in terms of the very disciplines placed at the vertices of the triangle of figure (a).[2] He viewed these, however, not as interacting domains of thought, but as in-

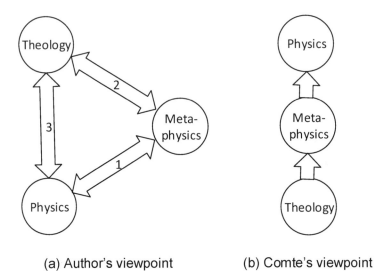

(a) Author's viewpoint   (b) Comte's viewpoint

dependent components of a hierarchy, through which, in the quest for *positive knowledge*, the Western mind passes successively, beginning, as shown in figure (b), with theology at the bottom, followed by an interlude of metaphysical speculation, and finally to physics at the top— the alleged crowning achievement of rational thought. Having arrived at this endpoint, the evolved intellect could now (according to Comte) discard metaphysics as meaningless and theology as mere superstition. Thus in Comte we discover the origin of *positivism*, the strict materialist view—one tacitly held by perhaps most of today's working scientists— that valid knowledge of the physical world is attainable only by adherence to the Enlightenment ideals of empiricism and scientific method.[3] We recognize too in Comte's analysis the notion, widespread in today's scientific community, that scientific progress can and should proceed without reference either to God or speculative philosophy.

The present volume thus stands in opposition to the prevailing materialist scientific worldview. Our aim is to show not only that God exists, but is directly responsible for the detailed, lawful structure of the physical world and along with it the possibility of life and mind. Admittedly, our approach to the problem of God's existence is on the formal side; and while aimed at the specialist, it should be readily followed by general readers with an appreciation for basic algebra and a willingness to contemplate complex diagrammatic material, particularly that presented in **Chapter 6**. If the argument advanced here is right, and despite its technical orientation, one can take heart in the knowledge that our Universe is by no means the meaningless, indifferent place it is too often said to be.

On a more personal side, the author admits that his credentials for publishing an interdisciplinary work such as the present one are far from overwhelming. His formal training consists of a doctorate in physics (University of Michigan, 1966), with an early published focus on holography, optical processing and optical self-imaging. Later, in industry, he turned to the design of multifocal ophthalmic lenses, and holds a number of patents in that field. Nothing in this background (except, perhaps, self-imaging) speaks directly to the metaphysical and theological issues pursued in this book. And yet, there are indirect links. For why in fact should there exist a field such as "physics" at all? Why should the physical world exhibit, not pure randomness, but observable regularities described by what we call "laws of nature"? Indeed, how do we know that the physical world we experience is real at all, and not a dream? These are the sorts of questions that have dogged the author throughout his career, questions not necessarily about physics as such, but why the world is the way it is. They were, moreover, questions not answered to his satisfaction in the existing literature, leading him to attempt to answer them on his own, and ending in the argument for God's existence presented here.

For completeness I should note that a somewhat truncated version of the manuscript for the present book was submitted sequentially to two professional journals for publication—one of these specially devoted to the intersection of science and religion. In both instances the submission was rejected without a word of comment or, perhaps, without even being read. This was disappointing, but not surprising. A similar fate met Reference [1] submitted serially to refereed journals of physics. In that earlier case, the reason for rejection had mainly to do with the work's metaphysical underpinnings—a hard sell in the light of today's scientific-materialistic worldview. In the present instance, I suspect an institutional bias prevailed against the intrusion of scientific method into traditional matters of faith. Fair enough. Figure (a) above depicts three separate disciplines interacting in the search for an ultimate Theory of

Everything—a TOE that includes God. I leave it to my readers to judge whether that goal has been achieved.

In undertaking this work the author has much benefited from discussions with Claude Labeeuw, Fr. David Severson, Fr. Matthew P. Huber, Fr. Michael Drury, Erin M. Green, Alex Menyhart, and Dr. Kristina Olsen.

Notes and references

[1] John T. Winthrop, *The Principle of True Representation: Mind, Matter and Geometry in a Self-Consistent Universe* (www.toplinkpublishing.com, 2019)

[2] Bruce Mazlish, "Comte, Auguste," in *The Encyclopedia of Philosophy*, Vol. 2, Paul Edwards, ed. (New York: Macmillan, 1967), 173-177. Actually, Comte refers to the third and final stage of his hierarchy as "the positive," which term is meant to encompass a full range of distinct sciences, e.g., astronomy, physics, chemistry, physiology. However, as everything physical ultimately reduces to physics, one might be forgiven for substituting, as I have done above, the term "physics" for Comte's "the positive."

[3] Nicola Abbragnano, "Positivism," in *The Encyclopedia of Philosophy*, Vol. 6, Paul Edwards, ed. (New York: Macmillan, 1967), 414-419.

Conventions and abbreviations

Four-dimensional (Minkowskian) space-time: M^4

Speed of light: c

Time in relativity: $x^0 \equiv ct$

Three-vector of position in space-time: $\mathbf{x} = (x, y, z)$

Four-vector of position in Minkowski M^4: $x^\mu = (x^0, \mathbf{x})$

Manifold of two infinite extra dimensions: (x^5, x^6)

Six-vector of position: $x^a = (x^0, \mathbf{x}, x^5, x^6)$

Three-vector of momentum: $\mathbf{p}$

Fifth component of momentum: p_5

Operators: $\hat{R}, \hat{\Omega}$

PTR = Principle of True Representation

LL = Law of Laws

CB = Conscious being

PART I

THE ARGUMENT

Chapter 1

Introduction

1.1 Existence

Part I of this book introduces a new argument for the existence of God. The guiding principle is to deal with the formal structure and meaning of existence itself rather than with the specifics of God's essential nature or with features of the physical world implying the handiwork of a Supreme Being. With this new approach the problem of proving God's existence differs little from that of proving the existence of anything else—the electron or Mt. Everest, for example. Moreover, it draws the question of God within the scope of scientific method, rendering the argument for God's existence—along with that of the external world—subject to experimental test. It reveals, too, as detailed in **Part II**, a picture of God's inner being—a structure remarkably consistent with that of the triune God of Christianity, and of mind-brain interaction in the conscious being.

1.1.1 *Types of existent*

To carry out our proof we are going to need a good definition of existence, where by "good" I mean something formal and testable, akin to a law of nature. This means, in other words, that our definition should have predictive value, with the potential empirically to be proved wrong. Although the philosophic literature has dealt at length on what it means to exist, it appears to offer nothing along the scientific-methodic lines we are looking for here. We are thus obliged to proceed on our own. I propose to begin by identifying the sorts of things that might be said to exist. Typically one divides ostensibly existing things into two types:[1, 2] things that exist objectively, independently of anyone's awareness of them (Type O) and those that exist subjectively, the content and formulations of mental activity (Type S). Examples of Type O existents are photons, doorknobs, and stars; and of Type S, percepts, dreams, and thoughts in general, including thoughts about

3

Unicorns and the positive integers.

Note that the Type O objects just mentioned are material in nature; they belong to a physical world potentially knowable by machine or sensory *observation*. But there exist also an *im*material Type O form, namely the laws of physics. While not made of matter, the laws are nevertheless objectively real because they remain in force whether or not we are here to talk about them. And of course there is still another possible *im*material Type O form, namely God. God, if he exists, belongs to an unobservable world directly knowable, if at all, not by observation but by *revelation*.

In the same way, Type S existents may take two forms: material and immaterial. The Type S examples given above are of the immaterial kind, the privileged mental content of conscious experience. The *neural correlates* of that mental content,[3] because residing in the brain, can be considered Type S existents in a material form. This may seem contradictory, because, being material, the neural correlates of conscious experience are observable by third-person observers, and consequently should—and *do*—count as Type O existents. However, they would not exist at all if not correlated with the unobservable, immaterial content of the mind. On that basis one may view the neural correlates of conscious experience as *ultimately* subjective and classifiable as Type S existent as well.

1.1.2 Appearance and reality

As we have just seen, our scheme of classification yields for both Type O and Type S existents two ontologically distinct principles: material and immaterial. The resultant four types of existent are usefully displayed in a two-by-two matrix, shown lightly-shaded in **Table 1.1**. This matrix is indeed comprehensive, a concise picture, as it were, of everything there is or could be. Thus far, however, we have merely identified separately the nature of the four elements of the matrix. We now want to consider the relationships between those elements. As we shall see, it is out of these relationships that a formal definition of existence ultimately emerges, leading to our proof of the existence of God.

Consider first the "Material" row of the matrix. Immanuel Kant (1724-

4

Table 1.1 Types of Existing Things		
Ontological Principle	Type	
	Objective (Type O)	Subjective (Type S)
Material	World (photons, doorknobs, stars)	Brain (Neural correlates of percepts, dreams, thoughts in general)
Immaterial	Laws of Physics God	Mind (Percepts, dreams, thoughts in general)

1804) said it was "a scandal to philosophy and to human reason in general" that we could not prove the existence of a world (Type O) outside ourselves (Type S).[4] Kant's reasoning was straightforward: What we claim to know about the world comes, not from the world itself, but from mere representations of it. In fact it could be that the representations we create are actually products of the imagination, as if in a dream. We have not proved otherwise. And so the problem of physical reality comes down to this: how do we show that our representations of the world are true; that they reflect accurately the reality of a world external to us, thereby demonstrating the existence of that world? None of this is new. We easily recognize here the classic problem of distinguishing between appearance and reality and of somehow reconciling them.[5] If we can do this, i.e., if we can find a testable relation between appearance and reality, we shall then have found the means of demonstrating, beyond a reasonable doubt, the reality of the external physical world.

Let us now look at the "Immaterial" row of the matrix. We see at once why it is so hard to prove the existence of God. For if we cannot—according to Kant—prove the existence of a tangible, visible world, how can we hope to prove the existence of an intangible, invisible God? We face again the problem of reconciling appearance and reality: in this instance the problem of finding a testable connection between internal revelation and the invisible, external God. Until we can do that we shall have failed in our quest to prove God's existence.

1.1.3 Ontological dualism

But our problems do not end there. A consideration of the *columns* of our two-by-two matrix yields two new ones. Let us start with the second or "Subjective (Type S)" column. We have two matrix elements to consider: mind and brain. The problem we face trying to relate them is not one of distinguishing between appearance and reality, but of reconciling an apparent causal interaction between two ontologically distinct things: immaterial mind and material brain. The interaction in question is called Cartesian dualism, a theory of the human person named naturally for its inventor, René Descartes (1596-1650).[6] The bulk of the neuroscience community, arguing as it does from a strict materialist viewpoint, rejects dualism out of hand. For most neuroscientists the mind is nothing but a property of the material brain (identity theory).[7] But this allegedly scientific attitude is almost certainly wrong.[8] For percepts and thoughts do exist in their own right and are not made of matter. The problem remains of determining what sort of world it can be that unites immaterial mind with material brain.

Let us turn now to the first or "Objective (Type O)" column of the matrix. Here we have two monumental elements to consider: God and the world. What is their relationship? In analogy with the dualism of brain and mind, it seems we may be looking at an *objective* form of Cartesian dualism, one wherein the material world could be considered the neural correlate of God. In fact it is this latter ostensible dualism, combined with a formalized approach to appearance and reality, which ultimately yields our new proof of God's existence.

1.2 Classic arguments for the existence of God

There is of course no current shortage of arguments for the existence of God. Indeed, the classic ontological, cosmological and teleological arguments, in their original and modified versions, together with critical analyses of their truth claims, form the basis of an entire branch of philosophy—the philosophy of religion.[9] And yet, influential as these arguments have been and continue to be, they have in common, in the writer's view, one and the same fatal, disqualifying flaw. Given our above list of existing things and their interrelationships, we are well positioned to identify this flaw, pointing the way to a new proof. There follows a brief review and critique of the three classic arguments.[10]

1.2.1 *Ontological argument*

Usually attributed to St. Anselm, Archbishop of Canterbury (1033-1109), the *ontological argument* begins by defining God in accordance to common understanding, namely, as "a being than which nothing greater can be conceived".[11] In other words God is, by definition, a being whose essential nature is one of maximal greatness: eternal, omnipotent, omniscient, immutable, and morally perfect. Let us denote this universal definition of God by G', where the prime attached to symbol G reminds us that G' refers only to a definition of God, not God himself. Now as St. Anselm puts it, what the individual contemplating God hears in reference to God is definition G'. Furthermore he "understands what he hears, and what he understands is in his understanding." Let us denote his understanding of definition G' by α'. Then for perfect agreement between the public definition and its mental instantiation, we have

$$\alpha' = G'. \tag{1.1}$$

This is the argument's first premise put in algebraic terms: God as an idea α' in the mind. St. Anselm then asserts that God "cannot exist in the understanding alone." For if he did, one could then conceive of a being even greater than that denoted by α', namely, one having real, extra-mental existence. Let this putatively greater being's representation in the mind be denoted by α''. We then have a second premise, asserting that the idea of a being that exists both in the understanding and in extra-mental reality is greater than the idea of one that exists in the understanding alone. In symbols, this second premise reads

$$\alpha'' > \alpha' . \tag{1.2}$$

Eliminating α' in this expression by means of Eq. (1), we obtain

$$\alpha'' > G' . \tag{1.3}$$

This says that we can conceive of a being greater than that which—by definition—nothing greater can be conceived—which is impossible. Therefore, the definition of God, G', as well as its perfect mental instantiation, α', must already entail the attribute of God's real, extramental existence. In other words, God necessarily exists. He does so for the simple reason that that which nothing greater can be conceived "cannot be conceived not to exist".[12]

1.2.2 *Cosmological argument*

Articulated in the *Physics* of Aristotle[13] (384/3-322 B.C.) and adopted 1.5 millennia later by St. Thomas Aquinas[14] (1225-1274) the *cosmological argument* begins empirically by assuming the existence of the physical world. It alleges that the world's current physical state W'_N is the result of a push by its proximate earlier state W'_{N-1}; that *that* state is caused by *its* proximate earlier state W'_{N-2}; and so on; see **Fig. 1.1**. But this causal regression must at some point stop, terminating at a first

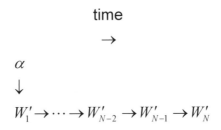

$$\text{time}$$
$$\rightarrow$$

$$\alpha$$
$$\downarrow$$

$$W'_1 \rightarrow \cdots \rightarrow W'_{N-2} \rightarrow W'_{N-1} \rightarrow W'_N$$

Fig. 1.1. Illustrating the cosmological argument. The world's current observed state W'_N arises from a sequence of earlier states W'_{N-m}, beginning with a first state W'_1, the initiator of which is God α, the First Cause. The initiating action of immaterial God is shown orthogonal to the temporal evolution of the material world.

state W_1', implying a First Cause. This First Cause, the necessary initiator of the world's existence, is God, α. The entire argument rests on the assumption that there exists an external world of real physical things and events. The prime attached to the symbol W_n' signifies an observed state, i.e., a machine-generated, mental representation of a corresponding state W_n of external reality.

But for completeness let us note the following. First, after Aristotle, St. Thomas argues that the causal regression cannot proceed to infinity, for if it did, no matter how far back in time one were to go, no initial state of the world would be found, making impossible the creation of a chain of subsequent states. Second, the transition from one state of the world to the next, starting with the current state, is felt both by the mover and the moved. (This is the analog of Newton's Third Law of Motion, that for every action there is an equal and opposite reaction.) The First Cause, however, is by definition immutable and thus unaffected in its bringing about the first step in the world's existence. For this reason St. Thomas refers to the First Cause as the Uncaused Cause or Unmoved Mover. This distinction between movers and Unmoved Mover means that God and the world differ ontologically, the latter material, the former immaterial. **Fig. 1.1** illustrates this crucial distinction, orienting God's creative action orthogonally to the temporal sequence initiated by him.

1.2.3 Teleological argument

Known also as the *argument from design* or the *analogical argument*, the *teleological argument* was presented in its classic form by the eighteenth-century philosopher William Paley.[15] Paley's analogical reasoning, depicted schematically in **Fig. 1.2,** runs as follows.

Empirically, one easily discerns the difference between a man-made artifact, such as a watch, and a naturally-occurring object such as a stone: the watch, on the evidence of its intricate internal movement, manifestly is the product of intelligent design (I. D.), assembled for the purpose of telling the time; in contrast, the stone presents no evidence of its having been brought into being for a specific purpose. But the

$$\left.\begin{array}{c} \text{I. D.} \\ \downarrow \\ \text{watch} \end{array}\right\} \Rightarrow \left\{\begin{array}{c} \alpha \\ \downarrow \\ W' \end{array}\right.$$

Fig. 1.2. Analogic structure of the teleological argument. An intricate, goal-directed mechanism such as a watch clearly must be the product of intelligent design (I. D.). But the natural world (W'), itself a kind of machine with interacting parts, also exhibits goal-directed behavior. It therefore must, like the watch, be the product of intelligent design, the designer in this case being God (α).

world at large (W') also shows goal-directed behavior. For with its vast inventory of living creatures, and whose component parts, e.g. the eye, act with the purpose of maintaining the creature, the world W' can itself be considered a machine, as if it were a great living watch. As such, because it manifests apparent purpose and because like effects have like causes, the world of Nature (Paley reasons) must be the handiwork of an intelligent designer. This designer is God, α. As in the cosmological argument, the teleological argument rests on the assumption that there exists an external world of real physical things and events. The prime attached to the symbol W' signifies the world as observed, i.e., a machine-generated mental representation of the corresponding world W of external reality.

1.3 Critique of the classic arguments

Now what are we to make of these arguments? Take first the ontological argument. As a matter of logic it strikes one as formally sound, conveying the notion that a being of unbounded perfection cannot be conceived not to exist. Nevertheless, it fails to convince. There are, I think, two reasons for this, one minor, the other more consequential. In the first instance, we note that the argument is entirely subjectivist. It never leaves the inner realm of understanding. This is shown by the primes affixed to each of the alphabetic symbols of Eqs. (1.1)-(1.3). Nowhere in these expressions is the objective God, whose existence is to be demonstrated, symbolically represented. What then becomes of God without at least one philosopher alive to argue for his existence?

But there is an even stronger case against the classical ontological argument. For suppose that extra-mental reality itself does not exist, that all is in the mind. Such a possibility was indeed entertained by René Descartes as the first step in his famous method of doubt, leading to the Cartesian *cogito*, "I think, therefore I am".[16] Because the Anselmian argument is all in the mind, whether there actually exists an external world is, as a matter of logic, irrelevant; the argument proceeds to its conclusion in either case. The ontological argument is thus exposed as incapable of proving what it claims to prove: for if there exists no external world, then no argument, irrespective of its formal power, can demonstrate the extra-mental existence of God.

Now what about the cosmological and teleological arguments? Unlike the ontological argument, neither makes use of the great-making attributes of a divine being. Instead, each focuses on perceived attributes of the natural world, the cosmological argument centering on causality, the teleological argument on the seeming presence of design in nature. However, as already noted, these are references to appearance, not reality, an ontological distinction indicated by the primed symbols in **Figs. 1.1** and **1.2**. And so, as in the case of the ontological argument, the two empirically-based arguments must fail if there happens to be no external world. Now because we know perfectly well (or think we do) that there exists an external world, such reasoning may strike one as at best philosophic scrupulosity. But it is not. Surely in a complete and convincing argument it is essential first to demonstrate the reality of an extra-mental world where God may actually exist.

1.4 The existential argument

All of which dictates the ultimate direction of this book. To argue convincingly for God's existence, I claim that we must first solve the *problem of the external world*.[17] This means demonstrating, in accordance to the philosophic assumption known as *metaphysical realism*,[18] that there exists a real, physical world external to the senses, a world that continues to exist when no one is looking. This effort, undertaken below, leads to the discovery of an algebraic form at once characterizing the structure of the entire natural world and signifying its objective existence. Let us for the moment denote this algebraic form—the world's signature of existence—by X. Significantly, form X, as a theory of nature, is empirically testable and has thus far stood up to every test to which it has been subjected—some of these quite severe. Thus we are able to prove, beyond a reasonable doubt, that there exists a real external world. Next we show that God, on the assumption that he exists, entails in overall form the same signature of objective existence, X. Now because logical forms, while arguably real, are not made of matter, the material world could not on its own have evolved its distinctive, immaterial signature form, X (or more precisely, its behavior as dictated by X). That form therefore must have originated elsewhere, namely in the immaterial, higher order of being called God, whose existence likewise is characterized by form X. One might say that in looking for clues as to why the world behaves as it does, one discovers God's fingerprint, X. In this way we see that God exists objectively, independently of human awareness. I propose to call this the *existential argument* for the existence of God.

Notes and references

[1] A. N. Prior, "Existence," in *The Encyclopedia of Philosophy,* Vol. 3, Paul Edwards, ed., (New York: Macmillan, 1967), 141-147.

[2] Eugene R. Fairweather, "Henry of Ghent," in *The Encyclopedia of Philosophy,* Vol. 3, Paul Edwards, ed., (New York: Macmillan, 1967), 475-476.

[3] David J. Chalmers, "What Is a Neural Correlate of Consciousness?" in *Neural Correlates of Consciousness,* Thomas Metzinger, ed., (Cambridge, MA: MIT Press, 2000), 17-39.

[4] Immanuel Kant, *Critique of Pure Reason,* Norman Kemp Smith, trans. (Houndmills, Basingstoke, Hampshire, UK: Palgrave Macmillan, 1929), corrections added to the Preface to the Second Edition, B xl.

[5] Bertrand Russell, *The Problems of Philosophy* (London: Oxford University Press, 1959), 7-16.

[6] René Descartes, *Meditations on First Philosophy*, John Cottingham, ed. (Cambridge, UK: Cambridge University Press, 1996), 50-62.

[7] Owen Flanagan, *The Science of the Mind*, 2nd ed. (Cambridge, MA: MIT Press, 1991), 57-59.

[8] Thomas Nagel, *Mind and Cosmos: Why the Materialist Neo-Darwinian Conception of Nature Is Almost Certainly False* (Oxford, UK: Oxford University Press, 2012), 37-42.

[9] "Philosophy of Religion," in *The Cambridge Dictionary of Philosophy*, Robert Audi, ed. (Cambridge, UK: Cambridge University Press, 1995), 607-611.

[10] Many readers will be familiar with these three classic arguments. I present them here in a somewhat mathematicised form for ready comparison with the existential proof introduced later in this book. I emphasize, too, the subjectivist nature of each of the arguments. For a detailed analysis of these and other classic proofs from a philosopher's perspective, see Edward Feser, *Five Proofs of the Existence of God* (San Francisco: Ignatius Press, 2017).

[11] St. Anselm., *Proslogium*, Ch. II, in *Anselm: Basic Writings*, S. N. Deane, trans. (Peru, IL: Open Court Publishing Co., 1962), 53-54.

[12] St. Anselm, Ch III.

[13] Aristotle, *The Basic Works of Aristotle*, Richard McKeon, ed. (New York: Modern Library, 2001), Physics, Book VII, 1 (241b 24).

[14] St. Thomas Aquinas, *Summa Contra Gentiles. Book One: God* (Notre Dame, IN: University of Notre Dame Press, 1975), Chapters 10-13.

[15] William Paley, *Natural Theology: Evidences of the Existence and Attributes of the Deity and Evidences of Christianity* (Oxford, UK: Benediction Classics, 2017), 3-9.

[16] René Descartes, *Discourse on Method* (New York: The Liberal Arts Press, 1956), Part IV.

[17] George Pappas, "Problem of the external world," in *A Companion to Epistemology*, Jonathan Dancy and Earnest Sosa, eds., (Malden, MA: Blackwell Publishing, 1992), 381-386.

[18] Panayot Butchvarov, "Metaphysical realism," in *The Cambridge Dictionary of Philosophy*, Robert Audi, ed. (Cambridge, UK: Cambridge University Press, 1995), 488-489.

Chapter 2

The problem of the external world

Our first task is to prove, beyond a reasonable doubt, the reality of the external world. To carry this out we shall follow the argument developed in the author's recently published book, *The Principle of True Representation*,[1] hereafter referred to as *PTR* (italicized). Because that argument is not widely known, I summarize it here in sufficient detail to support the objectives of this book. This will involve a little algebra, a feature not normally found in theological argument, but needed here to convey the testable content of signature X.

2.1 The unification of appearance and reality

Metaphysical realism assumes the reality of an external world of mind-independent physical *facts*. According to *representative realism* [2]—the species of realism we adopt here—what we observe in our experiments, and are supposed to interpret, are not facts of the physical world as such, but mere *representations* of the facts, generated by the sensory and laboratory apparatus. Consequently, on this view, because the external world is not directly observable, we have no way of knowing how closely the representations correspond to the facts, or even, for that matter, whether the facts actually exist. The *problem of the external world* is one of demonstrating that they do exist.

Now just as philosophers have presented arguments for the existence of God, so they have done for the existence of the external world.

- Famously, René Descartes argued that a perfect and infinite God—whose existence he established along Anselmian lines in the *Meditations*—is no deceiver, and thus bound not mislead us into believing in a world that does not exist.[3] "It follows that corporeal things exist."[4]
- An argument of Karl Popper's is even simpler. "I know that I am incapable of creating, out of my own imagination, anything as beautiful as the mountains and glaciers of Switzerland, or

15

even as some of the flowers and trees of my own garden. I know that ours is a world I never made."[5]

- Hilary Putnam, rephrasing a second argument of Popper's,[6] claimed that realism "is the only philosophy that doesn't make the success of science a miracle."[7]

Arguments such as these do agree with common sense, but in the end prove nothing. For integral to each is a conscious believer or observer. Take away the subjective, mental component and the arguments evaporate. To demonstrate the existence of God, one needs an objective and testable theory of the existence of the external world. There is just one way of achieving this: we have to establish a formal connection between the external world of facts and the empirical world of representations, and then see that it makes testable predictions. This is normal science, an example of the use of the scientific method, even though it begins with the assumption of metaphysical realism.

The required connection between the two worlds is readily obtained by treating the problem of the external world as a problem in communication theory. In the communications approach we view the representation as a message received from the external world of mind-independent facts. As depicted in **Fig. 2.1**, we take an arbitrary object O of the external world and let its behavior be fully specified by a certain descriptor χ. Further, let χ' denote a representation of χ obtained by machine observation of O. We seek connection between χ and χ'. In fact, there are two definable connections: one causal and the other denoting degree of correspondence. The first of these, which concerns the operational origin of the representation, brings into play a system (instrumental) operator $\hat{R}'$, a formal entity whose function is to act upon and project descriptor χ of the external world into the world of appearance, creating a representation (message) of the form

$$\chi' = \hat{R}'\chi. \tag{2.1}$$

In such a picture the representation χ' may or may not correspond exactly to the fact it represents. It may be corrupted in some way—

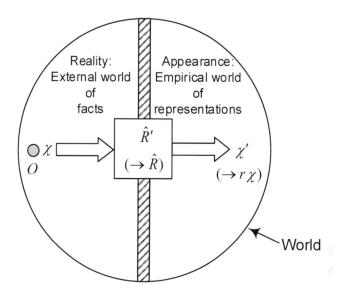

Fig. 2.1 Illustrating the problem of the external world and its solution. Instrumental operator $\hat{R}'$ operates on object O's descriptor χ, creating a representation $\chi' = \hat{R}'\chi$. In the special case that $\chi' = r\chi$, where r is a constant of unit magnitude, operator $\hat{R}'$ becomes objective space-time operator $\hat{R}$, yielding an exact representation $\chi' = \hat{R}\chi$. Eliminating χ' between the latter two equations yields the Law of Laws, Eq. (2.4) of the text.

missing fine detail, for example. In this expression the prime attached to the symbol χ' indicates the presence of possible error, and that attached to $\hat{R}'$ the instrumental (observational) source of that error. But now a special case arises, bringing us to the second form of connection. Suppose that appearances do not lie, and that the representation reproduces the fact exactly, up to a complex constant r of unit magnitude ($|r| = 1$). In symbols this correspondence condition reads

$$\chi' = r\chi. \tag{2.2}$$

The representation χ' may now be said to be *true*, as it corresponds exactly to the fact it represents. As a result we may remove the prime from operator $\hat{R}'$, yielding an objective space-time operator $\hat{R}$ and a correspondingly revised causal relation

$$\chi' = \hat{R}\chi \, . \tag{2.3}$$

On eliminating χ' between relations (2.2) and (2.3) we obtain an operator-theoretic relation defining the structure of an arbitrary fact χ of the external world:

$$\boxed{\hat{R}\chi = r\chi} \, . \tag{2.4}$$

Technically, (2.4) is an eigenvalue equation, with χ the eigendescriptor and r the eigenvalue. I call it the Law of Laws (LL) because, after putting it in terms of the dimensions of space-time, as outlined in **Sec. 2.2** below, it reproduces not only all known single-particle laws of physics, but yields significant enhancements of those laws, as well as new laws never seen before. In addition, and most importantly for us here, it forms a necessary condition for the existence of any physical object O, including the universe as a whole. It is our algebraic form X, the formal signature of existence of an external world of matter and energy.

From a foundational perspective our demand (2.2) for exact correspondence between fact and representation (up to constant r) amounts to a formal criterion of truth. In the light of its fundamental character I have chosen to call it the Principle of True Representation (PTR, unitalicized), and the LL (2.4) is a direct consequence of that principle. It implies that the natural world is self-representing, in that it manifests its own representation, with no conscious minds involved. Its principal effect is to replace the subjectivist measuring instrument characterized by operator $\hat{R}'$ with the objective, space-time operator $\hat{R}$, thereby bridging and unifying the worlds of appearance and reality. Self-representation thus emerges as the hallmark feature of existence. If the world could speak, it might do so in familiar Cartesian terms: "I self-represent, therefore I am." One is reminded too of Douglas Hofstader's notion of the Strange Loop: "The self comes into being at the moment it has the power to reflect itself."[8]

18

2.2 The world as a self-imaging process

Our task now is to show how the metaphysical Law of Laws, Eq. (2.4), manifests itself in the real physical world.[9] This will require a little technical space-time physics, unusual perhaps in metaphysics and theology, but essential to the development and credibility of our argument. We first note that, in overall form, the LL is identical to an already-known law governing the phenomenon of self-imaging in ordinary wave optics. Transposed to the realm of optics, Eq. (2.4) defines the structure of a monochromatic (single temporal frequency) scalar wave field χ which, under the action of space-time operator $\hat{R}$, propagates without dispersion (diffraction) along, say, the z-axis of 3-space. Such a field is said to be self-imaging, or non-diffracting, as in each cross section, by propagation alone, it reproduces itself up to a complex constant r of unit magnitude. Thus by analogy with optical self-imaging, we are invited to interpret descriptor χ in the LL as a self-imaging wave field, with operator $\hat{R}$ acting as wave propagator. On this interpretation, the physical world can be considered a self-imaging process, governed by the LL, Eq. (2.4).

Suppose we take at face value this interpretation of the LL. To get at its physical meaning and predictive content, we need to write it in terms of the variables of space-time. Because field χ is non-diffracting, its intensity $|\chi|^2$ has the same functional form in all cross sections Π of the propagating beam. These cross sections, however, cannot be the simple 2-D ones of optical self-imaging. Indeed, if the LL is to be a legitimate law of nature, one having the same form in all frames of reference, both χ and field operator $\hat{R}$ must depend on all four dimensions of ordinary space-time: (x^0, x, y, z). (In relativity the temporal dimension is spatialized by multiplying ordinary time t by the speed of light, c: $ct \equiv x^0$.) Each cross section Π, in other words, is to be identified with the full 4-D hyperplane, conventionally denoted M^4 (after Hermann Minkowski). But if cross section Π is already 4-D, then what possibly can be the direction of propagation? Clearly there must exist a fifth space-time dimension orthogonal to M^4 along which χ propagates. I call the new dimension x^5. It is flat, infinite and just as real as the

19

familiar four dimensions of M^4. It is not seen because the field intensity $|\chi|^2$ is independent of it. Although x^5 acts as an extra spatial dimension, it is metrically time-like, the significance of which feature is discussed below.

We are not yet done with extra dimensions. We know that the monochromatic optical field is driven by a single frequency associated with time. But in the case of the LL, ordinary time is embedded in cross-section M^4 and hence unavailable for energizing propagation along x^5. We conclude that, to get propagation, there must exist an extra time dimension as well. I call it x^6. Geometrically it is orthogonal to both M^4 and x^5 and is, like x^5, flat, infinite, and invisible. Although serving formally as a second time dimension, metrically x^6 is space-like. Together, x^5 and x^6 form a 2-D pseudo-Minkowskian space-time, $\bar{M}^2$, where the overbar reminds us that the metrical signatures are opposite to those of ordinary space and time. Thus total space-time, conveniently denoted as the product space $M^4 \times \bar{M}^2$, is $(4+2)$-dimensional.

2.3 Tests of the Law of Laws

As a general law of nature, the LL breaks down into separate laws, each distinguished by the forms of propagator $\hat{R}$ and wave function χ. Depending on its behavior under space-time transformations, χ may be of spinor, scalar, vector, or tensor form, while in each case wave propagator $\hat{R}$ represents and describes the particulate quantum belonging to χ.[10] Each separate law deriving from (2.4), having the form of a wave equation in M^4, has its own role to play in the description of the physical world. So, for example, the Dirac spinor describes the quantum states of fermions such as the electron and its neutrino. The scalar, vector and antisymmetric tensor wave functions describe the states of various kinds of boson; and so on. The presence in these equations of parameters coming from the extra dimensions leads to a number of testable predictions, placing the theory overall in peril of falsification. We give here four examples, selected from among many for their bearing on currently active areas of research. It should be understood the wave field χ entailed in each of these examples is a function of a *single* 6-vector of position, $(x^0, \mathbf{x}, x^5, x^6)$. Thus the LL is being tested here explicitly at the single-particle level. But as single particles do exist, and as complex physical structures (like atoms and molecules) are built out of single particles, it is reasonable to conclude that if we can show that single particles exist in reality, then composite structures do too.

- Superstring theory predicts the graviton, a spin-2 particle long conjectured to mediate the gravitational force.[11] But does the graviton actually exist? The gravitational field equations of Einstein originate from deep within (2.4) in the case where χ is the rank-4 Riemann-Christoffel curvature tensor, $R_{\alpha\beta\mu\nu}$. The field quantum associated with this gravity-generating tensor is not, however, the spin-2 graviton, but a new spin-1 particle I call the *riemann*. In other words *the graviton does not exist*, having been replaced by the riemann. Thus superstring theory, elegant as it may be, proves to be a false theory of nature.[12]

- In the $4+2$-dimensional space-time described above, all particles carry an extra (metrically time-like) momentum component p_5 associated with wave motion along x^5. Because x^5 is orthogonal to M^4, p_5 and ordinary 3-momentum **p** are separately conserved in any process. Then, according to the PTR, follows that
    - Proton decay is forbidden.
    - Neutrinoless double beta decay is likewise forbidden.
  Should either of these reactions be observed, the PTR and its associated LL would be falsified.[13]

- In the case that χ is a Dirac spinor, the LL generates for any given lepton (such as the electron or electron neutrino) *two* wave equations, one for probability amplitude, the other for electric charge amplitude. Utilizing these equations, the charge of each lepton is found to be proportional to the square of its (inertial) mass. Thus according to the PTR the (inertial) mass of the electrically-neutral neutrino is exactly zero, contradicting the now canonical (but theory-laden) result, inferred indirectly from neutrino oscillation experiments, that the neutrino has non-zero mass.[14] It should be noted that the best measurement thus far of

21

the neutrino's speed *in vacuo* is consistent with that of a particle of zero mass.[15]

- The M^4 hyperplane is everywhere perpendicular to dimension x^5. Therefore, according to the PTR, the universe as a whole must be flat, i.e., neither spherical nor saddle-shaped. Recent measurements of the cosmic microwave background indicate that the universe is indeed flat, within 0.4% margin of error.[16]

2.4 On the underlying significance of mathematics in the physical sciences

As we have just seen, the Law of Laws (2.4) is empirically falsifiable and thus qualifies as a genuine scientific theory. And as it has so far passed every test to which it has been submitted, we may reasonably conclude that, beyond a reasonable doubt, there does indeed exist an external world.

Now there is another piece of evidence for the existence of that world, one not yet mentioned, and perhaps a little surprising. Specifically this is the fact that the physical world's behavior can be described in mathematical terms. How is it that one can say how the physical world works with symbols and operations scribbled on the back of an envelope? In a famous essay entitled "On the Unreasonable Effectiveness of Mathematics in the Physical Sciences,"[17] Nobel physicist Eugene Wigner entertained this very question, but found it to be unanswerable. The essay begins, in fact, with this aim: to show

> "...that the enormous usefulness of mathematics in the natural sciences is something bordering on the mysterious and that there is no rational explanation for it."

and ends on this "more cheerful note":

> The miracle of the appropriateness of the language of mathematics for the formulation of the laws of physics is a wonderful gift which we neither understand nor deserve. We should be grateful for it and hope that it will remain valid in future research and that it will

extend, for better or for worse, to our pleasure, even though perhaps
also to our bafflement, to wide branches of learning.

In the light of our work here, it appears that an answer can now be given:
The world is describable mathematically for the simple reason that it
exists. For existence is marked by signature X, the Law of Laws, which
ultimately yields physical laws in mathematical form. The existence of
such laws, whose descriptive and predictive powers may be tested, thus
implies the existence of the very world to which they apply.

Notes and references

[1] John T. Winthrop, *The Principle of True Representation: Mind, Matter and Geometry in a Self-Consistent Universe* (www.toplinkpublishing.com, 2019), Chapter 2.

[2] Frank Jackson, "Representative realism," in *A Companion to Epistemology*, Jonathan Dancy and Earnest Sosa, eds. (Malden, MA: Blackwell Publishing, 1992), 445-448.

[3] René Descartes, *Meditations on First Philosophy*, John Cottingham, ed. (Cambridge, UK: Cambridge University Press, 1996), Fifth Meditation.

[4] René Descartes, Sixth Meditation.

[5] Karl R. Popper, *Realism and the Aim of Science*, W. W. Bartley, III, ed. (Totowa, NJ: Rowman and Littlefield, 1983), 84.

[6] Karl R. Popper, *Objective Knowledge*. (Oxford, UK: Oxford University Press, 1979), 40.

[7] Hilary Putnam, *Mathematics, Matter and Method* (Cambridge, UK: Cambridge University Press, 1975), 73.

[8] Douglas R. Hofstadter, *Gödel, Escher, Bach: An Eternal Golden Braid* (New York: Vintage Books, 1979), 709.

[9] Winthrop, *The Principle of True Representation*, Chapter 3.

[10] Winthrop, Chapters 4-8.

[11] *Superstrings: A Theory of Everything?*, P. C. W. Davies and J. Brown, eds., (Cambridge, UK: Cambridge University Press, 1988), 212. For a comprehensive, nontechnical review of string

theory, see Matthew Chalmers, "Stringscape,"
http://physicsworld.com/cws/article/indepth/30940.

[12]   Winthrop, *The Principle of True Representation*, 211-12.

[13]   Winthrop, 121-23.

[14]   Winthrop, 83-84, 108-10, 324-26.

[15]   Michael J. Longo, "Tests of relativity from SN1987A," Physical Review D 36, (1987): 3276.

[16]   Winthrop, *The Principle of True Representation*, 217.

[17]   Eugene P. Wigner, *Symmetries and Reflections* (Bloomington & London: Indiana University Press, 1967), 222-237. For some reflections on the Wigner essay, see S. M. Ulam, *Adventures of a Mathematician* (New York: Charles Scribner's Sons, 1976), 112, 277; Morris Kline, *Mathematics: The Loss of Certainty* (Oxford, UK: Oxford University Press, 1980), 349.

Chapter 3

The signature of God's existence

The first step in the existential argument is now complete. We have obtained an expression (2.4) signifying the existence of the external world and demonstrated its agreement with observation, confirming with high confidence the reality of the external world. The next step is to obtain an expression comparable to (2.4) signifying the real existence of God. As a formal matter this is perfectly straightforward. We have only to treat the problem of God's existence as we did that of the external world, namely, as a problem in communication theory. This means taking one's mental image or representation of God—on the assumption that God exists in reality—to be a received message, a message projected into the understanding by means of a dedicated system operator. However, having put the problem in these terms, we find ourselves faced with a grave difficulty: where, exactly, is this process of communication from God to the mind of man supposed to take place? What is the geometric setting? In the case of the problem of the external world, both communicating elements—facts and their machine-derived representations—consist of matter and energy and thus could be described within Minkowski M^4, supplemented by our two extra dimensions. But in the case of the problem of God, both God and mind are presumably immaterial, and so communication between them defies description in the context of ordinary space-time.

To see why this must be so, consider the faculty of mind. It operates in a privileged, subjective frame of reference, one philosophers refer to as the *first-person perspective*, or point of view.[1] But in ordinary 4-D space-time there can be no privileged frames of reference, as according to the Principle of Relativity,[2] one frame is as good as another for the formulation of the laws of physics. It follows that the phenomenon of conscious experience, occupying as it does a privileged frame of reference, lies beyond the reach of standard space-time physics.[3]

And then there is the problem of time. In physics time t is a dimension, akin to the three dimensions of space, and it is in terms of this parameter that one plots the motions of particles in 3-space—a static depiction called *block time* (or more commonly, the *block universe*). But the plotting of trajectories is not how one experiences time. Instead, time is experienced as a moving present moment, or *now*. Physics as standardly formulated, however, knows nothing of the moving present moment. And so again we see that conscious experience lies beyond the scope of ordinary space-time physics.[4]

Another aspect of time impacting the problem of God is this. In relativistic physics time t and energy E are complementary variables, often appearing together in the product form Et (time-harmonic vibration product) or $\Delta E \Delta t$ (uncertainty product). But God and mind, as claimed above, are by any reasonable definition immaterial categories of existence, consisting neither of matter nor its energy equivalent. Thus if God and mind exist, they do so in a space-time setting not parametrized by time t.

3.1 Dual space-time

Where, then, is this setting? For the answer we turn to the Law of Laws, Eq. (2.4), and for definiteness take descriptor χ to be a Dirac spinor. In this case the LL yields a 6-dimensional version of the Dirac equation— a quantum equation describing the behavior of single particles of matter such as electrons and protons. Now, to be a legitimate law of nature, this equation must remain form-invariant against circular rotations in the x^0-x^5 plane. Remarkably, we find that, under rotation, the equation retains its form for two angles only, namely $\pm 90°$. Let us for definiteness take for the rotation angle $-90°$. Then, because the angle is *finite*, not infinitesimal, the original frame K and the rotated frame K_D comprise two distinct realms of space-time, each physically inaccessible one from the other. We call K_D the *dual* of frame K, and the two frames superimposed, *dual space-time*; see **Fig. 3.1**. The upshot is that in dual space-time each physical event is described twice, once in K, the other in K_D. The Law of Laws, Eq. (2.4), is formulated in

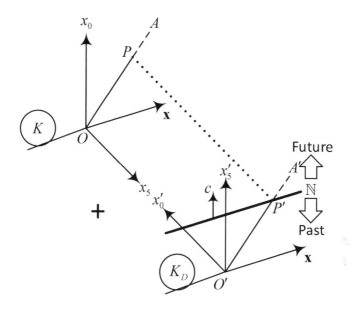

Fig. 3.1. Dual space-time consisting of superposed frames K and K_D. Dual frame K_D is produced by a counterclockwise rotation of frame K through an angle of $-90°$ about the **x** axis. As a result of the rotation, time x^0 is transformed into the quasi-spatial (metrically time-like) dimension x'^5. Superimposed, the two frames comprise *dual space-time* $K + K_D$. Line $O'A'$ in K_D is the *dual* of world line OA in K. The line labeled $\mathbb{N}$ in frame K_D represents the *moving present moment* or *now*. This line is in reality an infinite three-dimensional hyperplane oriented perpendicularly to the x'^5 axis and moving in a direction parallel to the x'^5 axis at the speed of light, c.

frame K. Transforming it by rotation into frame K_D, we have

$$\boxed{\hat{R}_D \chi_D = r \chi_D}, \tag{3.1}$$

where χ_D and $\hat{R}_D$ are rotationally-transformed versions of their counterparts in (2.4). Factor r is unaffected by the transformation because it is a constant. Notably the overall form of the LL is the same in both frames. Equation (3.1) is the signature of existence of the external world as viewed from the perspective of dual frame K_D. We could call it form X_D.

Let us now write down the two coordinate transformation equations taking frame K into K_D, assuming a rotation angle of $-90°$. One of these is $x'^0 = -x^5$, whereas the other more interesting one reads

$$x'^5 = x^0 = ct, \qquad (3.2)$$

where x'^0 and x'^5 are the new (rotated) coordinates, t is ordinary time and c is the speed of light. Equation (3.2) is an equation of motion. It describes, within K_D, a line of infinite extent (actually a 3-D hyperplane) oriented perpendicularly to the x'^5 axis and moving in a direction parallel to it at the speed of light. This line, labelled $\mathbb{N}$ in **Fig. 3.1**, is none other than the moving present moment or *now*. It is now easy to understand how the world is experienced temporally. In the figure, OA is the world line (space-time track) of a particle in K and $O'A'$ is its dual in K_D. The moving present moment $\mathbb{N}$ intersects dual world line $O'A'$ at point P', creating for the conscious observer in K_D (should one be present!), looking at P', the twin illusions of particle motion parallel to the **x** axis and of time passing.

We should emphasize that events in K_D—the duals of events in K—are parametrized, not by time t, but by the fifth quasi-spatial coordinate x'^5. This means that the moving present moment $\mathbb{N}$ is a line of simultaneity, as all dual events intercepted by it occur at the same universal time t, in accordance to Eq. (3.2). In turn this means that, in K_D, all points of the quantum-mechanical state vector—an instance of descriptor χ_D of Eq. (3.1)—are in instantaneous causal contact, no matter how far apart spatially they may be, thereby resolving the paradox of state vector collapse, and yielding to the concept of dual space-time scientific credibility.[5]

The geometric setting for connection between God and a knowing mind is now clear. As K_D is inaccessible from frame K, it offers the possibility of a first person perspective. It contains in addition the moving present moment. Thus K_D not only forms the natural home of conscious experience, but of God as well, for if God were somewhere else, no connection between God and mind could take place. Owing to their mutual confinement in K_D, God and mind are revealed as ontologically equivalent categories of existence, distinct from matter and energy.

3.2 Formal signature of God's existence

Just as the problem of the external world begins with the assumption of metaphysical realism, the *problem of God* begins with the assumption of theological realism: God's existence, if he exists at all, is realized in frame K_D. Let us denote God's real being in K_D—his (immaterial) essence—by α, the analog of physical descriptor χ. Further, let us denote by α' an understanding or knowledge of α acquired by the knowing subject. As in the problem of the external world, we seek two connections between the reality and the representation, one causal, the other an expression of degree of correspondence. The first of these relates to how an image of God gets into the understanding. We picture it here, as shown in **Fig. 3.2,** as the effect of a system operator, $\hat{\Omega}'$, acting

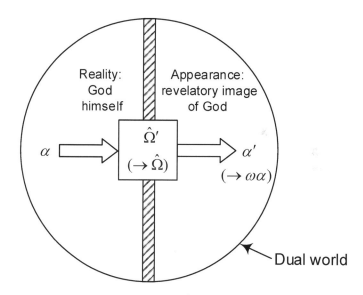

Fig. 3.2. Illustrating the problem of God and its solution. Revelation operator $\hat{\Omega}'$ operates on God's essential being α, creating a mental representation $\alpha' = \hat{\Omega}'\alpha$. In the special case that $\alpha' = \omega\alpha$, where ω is a constant of unit magnitude, operator $\hat{\Omega}'$ becomes objective operator $\hat{\Omega}$, yielding an exact representation $\alpha' = \hat{\Omega}\alpha$. Eliminating α' between the latter two equations yields God's signature, Eq. (3.6) of the text.

upon α and projecting it into the mind of the knower, creating there a mental representation of the form

$$\alpha' = \hat{\Omega}'\alpha. \tag{3.3}$$

Clearly operator $\hat{\Omega}'$, in contrast to instrumental operator $\hat{R}'$ defined earlier, can have nothing to do with normal powers of observation. In particular it cannot represent the action of conventional laboratory apparatus; for no physical mechanism, including the organs of sense, can detect the presence of an immaterial God. Operation $\hat{\Omega}'$ is transcendental in nature, not instrumental; it stands for *revelation*, the only known—if hypothetical—means of attaining direct knowledge of God.

Now no finite being, one such as ourselves, can hope to achieve by revelation a perfect understanding or experience of God. The primes attached to the symbols α' and $\hat{\Omega}'$ are meant to signal the imperfect, subjective nature of that which they symbolize. There exists in principle, however, at least one being capable of achieving perfect knowledge of God, namely, God himself. In this unique case the representation reproduces exactly the reality, thereby yielding our required second connection[6]

$$\alpha' = \omega\alpha, \tag{3.4}$$

where ω, like constant r above, denotes a complex constant of unit magnitude. We may now remove the prime from revelation operator $\hat{\Omega}'$, yielding the objective projection operator $\hat{\Omega}$ and a revised causal relation

$$\alpha' = \hat{\Omega}\alpha. \tag{3.5}$$

Eliminating α' between (3.4) and (3.5), we obtain the single relation

$$\boxed{\hat{\Omega}\alpha = \omega\alpha}. \tag{3.6}$$

If God exists, this operator-algebraic form is his signature. Like the LL

(2.4)/(3.1), Eq. (3.6) is the result of applying the PTR—here expressed by the correspondence condition (3.4)—to the problem of God. The principal effect of that condition is to replace the finite mind seeking revelatory knowledge of God with the self-knowing mind of God himself. It implies that, like the physical world, God is a self-consistent, self-representing being, one characterized by three interacting elements, α, α', and projection operator $\hat{\Omega}$. The interpretation of this trinity of elements in conventional Scriptural terms is discussed below in **Chapter 5**.

Notes and references

[1]   John R. Searle, *The Rediscovery of the Mind* (Cambridge, MA: MIT Press, 1992), 116-18.

[2]   Albert Einstein, *Relativity: The Special and the General Theory*, Robert W. Lawson, trans. (New York: Crown Publishers, Inc., 1961), 13-15, 60.

[3]   John T. Winthrop, *The Principle of True Representation: Mind, Matter and Geometry in a Self-Consistent Universe* (www.toplinkpublishing.com, 2019), 5-7.

[4]   Winthrop, 461-463.

[5]   Winthrop, pp. 443-453.

[6]   A young philosopher anticipates this relation: "God alone is capable of loving God." Simone Weil, *Waiting for God* (New York: Harper Perennial, 2009), 80.

Chapter 4

The existential argument

4.1 Seven steps

With the foregoing preparation the existential argument for the existence of God now finally can be made. There are seven steps.

1. Algebraic form (2.4)—the Law of Laws in frame K—at once defines the overall structure of the external world and signifies its real existence. **(Secs. 2.1-3)**

2. Algebraic form (3.1) — the Law of Laws transformed by rotation into dual frame K_D—defines the structure of the external world viewed from the perspective of K_D, the space-time setting in which connection between God and mind can occur. **(Sec. 3.1)**

3. The Law of Laws is confirmed empirically in both frames K and K_D, corroborating the theory and proving, beyond a reasonable doubt, the existence of the external world. **(Secs. 2.3, 3.1)**

4. Algebraic form (3.6), formally identical to Eq. (3.1)—the Law of Laws transformed to frame K_D—at once defines the overall structure of God and, should he exist, signifies his real existence. **(Sec. 3.2)**

5. The Law of Laws in either its original or rotated form, while perfectly real, is not made of matter, and thus could not have originated in the material world.

6. The Law of Laws must therefore have been imposed upon the world by other means, namely by God, whose (immaterial) formal structure Eq. (3.6) is isomorphic (similar in form) to that of the external, dual material world, Eq. (3.1).

7. Therefore, as the external, dual material world has been shown empirically to exist, so too must God exist.

Figure 4.1 presents the argument in diagrammatic form. In this figure, numbers 1-7 identify the steps of the argument as set forth above. Double-shafted arrows connect signatures of existence, forming the

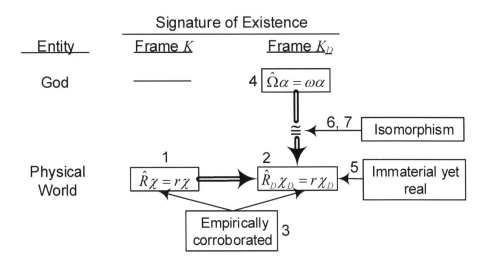

Fig. 4.1 Illustrating the existential argument. Numbers 1-7 identify the steps in the argument, and the double arrows, the basic logic flow. The material world's algebraic signature of existence (1) in frame K transforms by rotation in the x^0-x^5 plane into its corresponding signature of existence (2) in dual frame K_D. Both forms are (3) empirically corroborated. Algebraic form (4) signifies God's existence, if he in fact exists. As the material world's signature of existence is (5) immaterial yet real, it can only have come from God, whose signature is (6) isomorphic to that of the material world. Therefore (7) God exists.

basic logic flow of the argument. Text boxes 3 and 5 refer to subsidiary conditions integral to the argument, and text box with arrow 6, 7 identifies the logic operation leading to the argument's conclusion. It is worth noting that the existential argument involves immaterial yet objectively-real entities only—the contents of the first box in the second row of the shaded matrix of **Table 1.1**. It references neither material objects nor the mental contents of knowing beings.

The existential argument for God's existence—owing to the need first to prove the existence of the external world—is obviously more complicated than any of the three classic arguments discussed in **Sec. 1.2** of this book. Nevertheless, there are points of overlap. Consider the ontological argument. It begins with the assumption of exact correspondence between an acknowledged definition of God (G') and one's image of it (α') in the understanding, as expressed by Eq. (1.1). In form this equation resembles Eq. (3.4), the PTR applied to the problem of God. The difference in meaning between the two equations is that, whereas (3.4) expresses the unification of subjective appearance and objective reality, Eq. (1.1) merely equates two subjective representations—a definition of God and one's mental image of it. Nor does the ontological argument offer any mechanism, analogous to that expressed by Eq. (3.3), for projecting an image of the God of reality into the understanding. Consequently the ontological argument, in failing to make contact with the objective God, leaves his existence unproved.

As for the cosmological and teleological arguments, both **Figs. 1.1** and **1.2,** as in **Fig. 4.1,** show a causal arrow pointing down from God to the world. But here the similarity between the existential and two classic arguments ends. For the existential argument is not a first-cause argument; nor is it an argument from design. Instead it argues from the fact that God's signature of existence is isomorphic to that of the world—an external world whose existence is confirmed empirically. In both of these classic arguments the world to which God points may or may not even exist. Thus neither succeeds in proving God's existence.

4.2 God and scientific method

The Law of Laws (2.4)/(3.1) is in essence a theoretical construct, one whose claim to truth demands confirmation by experimental test. The theory that there exists an external world is, in other words, like all scientific proposals, subject to corroboration by way of the scientific method—a corroboration we claim already to have achieved. Now the signature of God's existence (3.6) is isomorphic to that of the world, (2.4)/(3.1); this is step 6 in the existential argument. In formal terms, $(3.6) \cong (2.4)/(3.1)$. It follows that the existential argument for God's existence is an empirically falsifiable construct. For if the LL (2.4)/(3.1) were to be empirically falsified, logical form (3.6) would then have nothing to be isomorphic to, invalidating the existential argument. In this way we see that the existential argument for God's existence is, like that of the physical world, and despite God's immaterial nature, subject to empirical corroboration and is falsifiable. Note, however, that it is only the argument, not God himself, that is falsifiable.

4.3 God, time, and the world

Premise 2 in the existential argument posits the existence of dual frame K_D. This is not a step in logic. Rather it identifies the region of space-time available for occupation by mind and God, the physical setting of the argument. But it yields something more as well: namely, a heightened understanding of God's relationship to the world. First, it shows that God lives *somewhere* within the geometry of space-time, not, as is sometimes imagined, beyond or outside it. Second, it suggests that, because God is in K_D, he may experience the world temporally much as we do: from moment to moment, and with at any given moment simultaneous apprehension of spatially separated (dual) events. In addition, he has contemporaneous access to and knowledge of all past events of the world, as these are frozen in the past dual block universe. And finally, because God is immaterial and thus excluded from frame K, his confinement to frame K_D—a place free of energy and time t—refutes *pantheism*, a false philosophy held by Spinoza, Hegel and others that conflates God and the world.[1]

4.4 Reality of the Law of Laws

Premise 5 makes two assertions. First, the LL, though immaterial, is nonetheless real. This must be so, as by definition the LL constitutes an objective, defining characteristic of the physical world, namely its existence. It has been here from the beginning and, unlike the Pythagorean theorem, say, will not go away when we do.

Second, premise 5 asserts that the LL, *because* immaterial, could not have arisen on its own in a material world. The world of matter and energy could not, in other words, have decided to represent itself, as if it were conscious. Nor could the LL have arisen as an "emergent" property of nature, for, as the signature of existence, it applies not only to the universe as a whole, but equally to its minutest constituents. It is not as if existence could emerge out of some lesser version of itself.

Absent these two assertions, one could not properly lay claim to conclusions 6 and 7.

Reference

[1]   Alasdair MacIntyre, "Pantheism," in *The Encyclopedia of Philosophy*, Vol. 6, Paul Edwards, ed. (New York: Macmillan, 1967), 31-35.

PART II

CONSEQUENCES

Chapter 5

The image of God

Scripturally, it is said that "God created man in his image;" (Genesis 1:27).[1] On the present account, it is not only man, but Nature as a whole that is made in God's image. The formal connection between material Nature and immaterial God is easily seen by comparing the communication-theoretic pictures of the physical world, **Fig. 2.1**, and of God, **Fig. 3.2**. Each consists of an input, an output, and a projecting mechanism operating between them.

Remarkably, the purely technical depiction of God of **Fig. 3.2** translates into an image consistent with the triune God of Christianity. To see this we have only to find textual equivalents within the Gospel of Eqs. (3.4) and (3.5), as these are the theoretic elements illustrated by **Fig. 3.2** and which, when combined, yield God's signature of existence, Eq. (3.6).

Consider first Eq. (3.5). As noted earlier, this relation describes a particular causal action—the projection of God's real being into the world of representations. Its Gospel equivalent is eloquently expressed by John 1:1:[2] "In the beginning was the Word; the Word was in God's presence, and the Word was God." Here the Word is Jesus, the Son of God. He is the Word because, like all words, he is a projection of the speaker, in this case God the Father. In short, the Son is a representation (α') of the Father (α). Further, in 1 Corinthians 2:10 we read[3] "Yet God has revealed this wisdom to us through the Spirit." Here we learn finally the meaning of the objective projection operator $\hat{\Omega}$: if operator $\hat{\Omega}'$ in Eq. (3.3) stands for subjective revelation, then, according to Saint Paul, operator $\hat{\Omega}$ in Eq. (3.5) represents the action of the *Holy Spirit*. Words in general require a projecting force and intervening medium, carrying them from speaker to listener. In the triune God, the Holy Spirit provides both force and medium.

As for Eq. (3.4), in John 10:30 we read "The Father and I are one."[4] And in Colossians 1:15, "He is the image of the invisible God, the first-born of all creatures."[5] Here we have clear statements in the New Testament itself of the PTR applied to the problem of God: the unification of God the Son (α') and God the Father (α). These words of Jesus, as reported by Saint John, and of Saint Paul, express Eq. (3.4) to perfection.

In sum, we have established a one-to one correspondence between the three active elements of God's communication-theoretic signature, Eq. (3.6), and the three persons comprising the three-in-one God of Christianity, namely: α = God the Father, α' = God the Son, and $\hat{\Omega}$ = God the Holy Spirit. **Figure 3.2** can now be redrawn as **Fig. 5.1(a)**, expressing the communication-theoretic picture of God in terms of the three persons of the God of Christianity. *The triune Christian God is thus revealed as a self-representing being, and one who, in virtue of the existential argument, truly exists, beyond a reasonable doubt.*

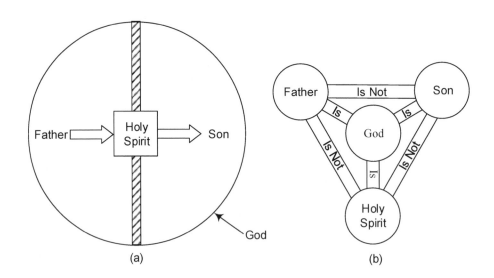

(a)   (b)

Fig. 5.1 The three-in-one structure of God. **(a)** According to the communications-theoretic structure of **Fig. 3.2**, its three elements identified in Scriptural terms. **(b)** According to the Athanasian Creed.

Although we have managed to *derive* an image of the Christian God, in fact the three persons of the Holy Trinity are nowhere bound together as one God within the Gospel itself. Instead, according to Church tradition, the dogma of the Holy Trinity arose by way of revelation, the main symbols of which are the Apostles', the Nicene, and the Athanasian Creed.[6] The latter creed is of particular interest for us here, as it presents explicitly the three persons of the Trinity as coequal and coeternal.[7] A well-known image of the Holy Trinity derived from the Athanasian Creed is shown in **Fig. 5.1(b)** for ready comparison with the image of God derived from the existential argument. According to the Athanasian Creed:[8]

- Each of the three persons of the Trinity—Father, Son, and Holy Spirit—is uncreated, limitless, eternal, and omnipotent—more or less the divine attributes underlying the formulation of the ontological argument; attributes denoting "a being than which nothing greater can be conceived." In contrast, the existential argument unfolds irrespective of God's essential nature. In that argument one need only assume the mind of God to be of sufficient capacity to comprehend itself, however great that may be; see Eq. (3.6). Of course it is a very great mind indeed, as it ensures, owing to its form, not only its own existence, but that of the entire physical world.

- The three persons of the Trinity are separate but equal, as indicated by the "Is Not" connectors of **Fig. 5.1(b)**; and although each is God, expressed by the "Is" connectors of that figure, together they form a unity of *one* God, the three-in-one God of Christianity. The image of God derived from the existential argument is likewise of three-in-one form. The three persons comprising it are also separate but equal, as suggested diagrammatically by the cross-hatched barrier and boxed Holy Spirit of **Fig. 5.1(a)**; for owing to their dynamic relationship, none of the three can survive, or has meaning, without the other two.

- The Father is neither created nor begotten; and the Son is neither created nor begotten, but of the Father alone. The images of the

43

first two persons of the Trinity deriving from the existential argument are thus in close agreement with those specified by the Creed. For the dictum that the Son is of the Father alone is a distinct foreshadowing of the PTR, as expressed by Eq. (3.4).

- The Holy Spirit is neither created nor begotten, but proceeding from the Father alone (Eastern Orthodox) or from both the Father and the Son (Western Church). The image of the Holy Spirit implied by the existential argument is consistent with either of these interpretations. For in the existential argument, the Holy Spirit plays a role analogous to that of a system operator, an intermediary who projects an image of the Father into the space of representations, the Father's image being the Son himself. In John 14:26,[9] Jesus tells Judas (not Judas Iscariot) that "...the Paraclete, the Holy Spirit whom the Father will send in my name, will instruct you in everything...". The Paraclete is the divine intercessor, one who, according to the existential argument, intercedes even within the Holy Trinity itself. "The Spirit scrutinizes all matters, even the deep things of God." (1 Corinthians 2:10)[10]

Notes and references

[1] *The New American Bible* (New York: Catholic Book Publishing Co., 1970). Hereafter referred to as *TNAB*.

[2] *TNAB*

[3] *TNAB*

[4] *TNAB*

[5] *TNAB*

[6] Phillip Schaff, *The Creeds of Christiandom*, Vol. I (Grand Rapids, MI: Baker Books, [1877] 1998), 12.

[7] Schaff, 34-32.

[8] Schaff, Vol. II, 66-73.

[9] *The New American Bible*

[10] *TNAB*

Chapter 6

God and conscious experience

In *Sec. 3.1* it was argued that both God and mind occupy and are confined to the same hidden domain of space-time, dual frame K_D. Could this mean that God and mind—or more generally, conscious experience—are somehow connected? The answer is that they almost certainly are. To confirm this we are going to derive the general structure of the conscious being and then show how it imitates precisely the self-referencing structure of the triune God. This close structural agreement is unlikely to be accidental. It implies that the dualist mind-brain structure of the conscious being is of transcendental origin. A more detailed account of the conscious being herself will be found in **Ref. [1]**.

6.1 Mind-brain dualism

6.1.1 We take as given the reality of space-time frame K and dual frame K_D. The two frames, when superimposed, comprise dual space-time, $K + K_D$.

6.1.2 It is then natural to assume that if material brain exists in K, and its dual in K_D, then immaterial mind, if it exists at all, does so in K_D. This is the hypothesis of mind-brain dualism, as dictated by dual space-time. Our immediate task is to demonstrate empirically the truth of that hypothesis.

6.2 Consciousness

6.2.1 We define consciousness operationally as "the capacity of the individual or Self (Ego) to read, understand and act upon internal representations of external events".[2] Here "reading" and "acting" refer, respectively, to the mental operations of *perception* and *will*.

45

6.2.2 Consciousness is linked to and facilitated by the moving present moment, or *now*. Conscious understanding occurs *within* that moment, whereas perception occurs in the *past* and will in the *future* of that moment, as discussed below. As the temporal now exists in K_D only, it is clear that understanding, perception, and will also exist in K_D only.

6.3 Structure of the conscious being

6.3.1 As consciousness entails both "internal representations" and "external events", the structure of the conscious being (CB) cannot be discussed or understood scientifically apart from the structure of space-time.

6.3.2 **Figure 6.1** depicts the basic elements of the CB and flow of information between them. As shown, in accordance to mind-brain dualism, the CB's brain occupies space-time frame K, while her brain dual and mind occupy frame K_D. The cross-hatched barrier between the two frames reminds us of the private, first-person status of the conscious mind: because it is confined to K_D, the CB's mind is inaccessible to third-person observers located in frame K. Of course, hints about what is going on in the mind might be obtained for the observer indirectly by attending to the subject's body language or measurements of her brain activity.

6.3.3 As shown in **Fig. 6.1**, the mental operations *perception*, *will*, and *understanding* occur within dual frame K_D. These are facilitated by the four operators T, T^{-1}, U^{-1}, and U, working in conjunction with the moving present moment, as discussed below.

6.3.4 The operating structure of a robot, **Fig. 6.2**, differs markedly from that of the CB. The impenetrable barrier between frames K and K_D precludes endowment of this—or any—man-made machine with the first-person, mental faculties of perception, will, and understanding. And this includes the computer, no matter how complex or powerful. A man-made machine, in other words, in principle cannot be rendered conscious. Curiously, in rejecting dualism, contemporary neuroscience chooses—wrongly—to model human cognitive function after that of a robot.

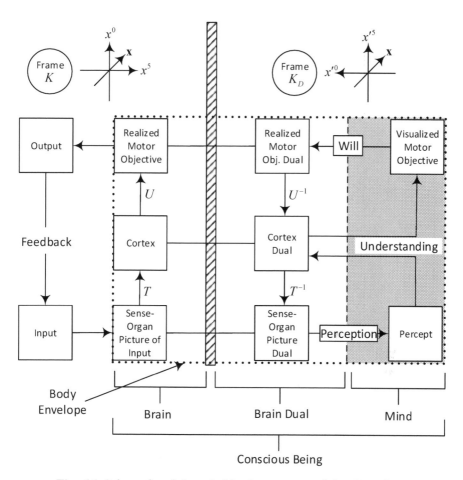

Fig. 6.1 Schematic of the mind-brain structure of the Conscious Being. In accordance to mind-brain dualism, the Brain occupies space-time Frame K, while the Brain Dual and Mind occupy Frame K_D. Conscious mental operations Understanding, Perception, and Will are achieved as described in the text, with operators, T. T^{-1}, U^{-1}, and U, working in conjunction with the moving present moment (now).

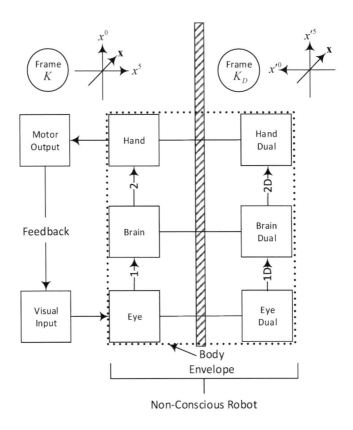

Fig. 6.2 Operational structure of the Non-Conscious Robot, for comparison with that of the Conscious Being, **Fig. 6.1**. The robot has been programmed to perform a simple task, such as picking up a pencil. Information about the robot's current hand position (Motor Output) relative to the pencil is received by the eye and sent along path 1 to the "Brain", which then—after noting the difference between the current and desired hand positions—sends instructions along path 2 to a motor control device for appropriate adjustment of the hand position. This is a negative feedback machine. The eye, brain, and hand duals in Frame K_D, as well as the pathways 1D, 2D between them, are, in the case of the robot, completely redundant and thus may be omitted from its functional description. As suggested by the cross-hatched barrier, Frame K_D is inaccessible to the builder of a robot, and no robot can be made conscious.

6.4 Perception

6.4.1 Perception in the conscious being is perhaps best explained by way of the visual experience, vision being the dominant sensory modality. We place ourselves to the right of the CB's body envelope of **Fig. 6.1** and view the apparatus and operations internal to it in a direction parallel to the x'^0 axis. We are thus looking at a normal projection of frame K_D and its contents onto frame K and *its* contents.

6.4.2 **Fig. 6.3** presents three cross sections of the CB's Mind and Brain from the vantage point just described. Reading from left to right: a first section cuts through the Brain in frame K, a second one through the Brain Dual in frame K_D, and a final one through the Mind, also in K_D.

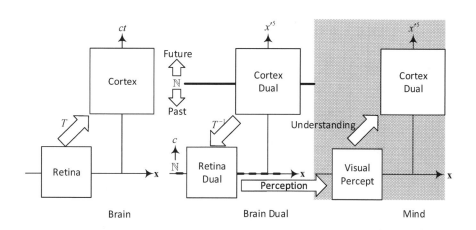

Fig. 6.3 Illustrating perception in dual space-time. Shown are three cross sections through the Conscious Being's mind and brain depicted in **Fig. 6.1**, as viewed from the right in a direction parallel to the x'^0 axis. Visual information flows from left to right, from Brain to Mind.

6.4.3 Perception in dual space-time works from left to right in **Fig. 6.3**. There are three steps. (a) It begins with an image formed on the retina by the cornea and crystalline lens of the eye. This image, converted to electrical pulses, proceeds by electrochemical pathway to the visual cortex, an operation indicated in the figure by operator T. Within the cortex as a whole, this image is analyzed with respect to data stored already in memory and then later understood. (b) The world lines of this activity in the Brain are automatically captured and preserved as a permanent block in the Brain Dual owing to the movement of the present moment $\mathbb{N}$ as shown. The causal relationship between the cortex dual and the retinal image dual, the latter existing now in *past* block time, is here indicated by operator T^{-1}. Operation T^{-1} occurs automatically and replaces image reconstruction by signal synchrony thought by most neuroscientists to occur within the cortex itself. (c) The act of perception, as indicated by the "Perception" arrow, consists of apprehending within the Mind itself the retinal image dual. In other words, the image dual projected into the mind becomes the visual percept. It is at this point, as indicated by the "Understanding" arrow, that understanding of the percept's import for the CB occurs.

6.5 Will

6.5.1 The will is perhaps best understood by way of conscious motor control. We again place ourselves to the right of the CB's body envelope of **Fig. 6.1** and view the apparatus and operations internal to it in a direction parallel to the x'^0 axis.

6.5.2 As in **Fig. 6.3, Fig. 6.4** presents three cross sections of the CB's mind and brain from the vantage point just described: a first section cuts through the Brain in frame K, a second one through the Brain Dual in frame K_D, and a final one through the Mind, also in K_D.

6.5.3 The action of the will is readily conceived as perception run in reverse. Thus in dual space-time, volition works from right to left in **Fig. 6.4**. As in perception, there are three steps. (a) Just as perception *ends* with understanding, the conscious being's act of will *begins* with understanding. What she understands is the wish to move of a part of the body, a flick of the wrist, for example. Accordingly, at the moment of understanding, a visualized motor objective is projected instantaneously into the *future* of that moment, the latter represented in

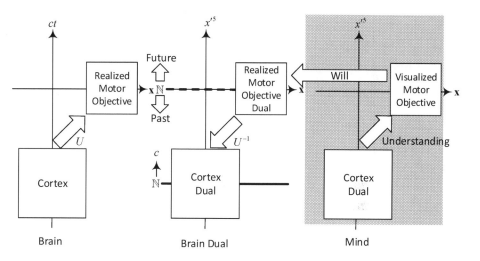

Fig. 6.4 Illustrating action of the will in dual space-time. Shown are three cross sections through the Conscious Being's mind and brain depicted in **Fig. 6.1**, as viewed from the right in a direction parallel to the x'^0 axis. Volitional information flows from right to left, from Mind to Brain. Will thus can be conceived as perception run in reverse; cf. **Fig. 6.3**.

Fig. 6.4 by the solid-line present moment $\mathbb{N}$ passing through the cortex dual. (b) The act of will, a mind-brain interaction indicated by the "Will" arrow, is completed by instantaneous projection of the visualized motor objective into the brain dual, where it forms the dual of the realized motor objective. Because it lies in the future, the realized motor objective dual cannot be detected by third-person observers. Moreover, at that same moment, the future world lines of the motor cortex dual are automatically configured in exact causal correspondence to the realized motor objective dual. This latter step is represented in the figure by operator U^{-1}. (c) Finally, the present moment $\mathbb{N}$, moving at the speed of light, scans the now-established future world lines of the motor cortex dual, giving rise to the realized motor objective, a now-observable flick of the wrist, for example. This realization operation, which ends with $\mathbb{N}$

in the dashed-line position shown, is represented by operator U in the figure.

6.5.4 Two additional points relating to the will are worth noting. First, while the Understanding and U^{-1} operations are inaccessible to machine observation—their being confined to dual frame K_D, and in the case of U^{-1} existing in the future—operation U is perfectly detectable by electromyogram in frame K. Second, and most importantly, *creation of the visualized motor objective occurs without expenditure of energy.* That is because in frame K_D, energy E, like ordinary time t, does not exist, having been replaced by a time-like fifth momentum, p_5. Thus the standard neuroscientific objection to mental interaction with the brain[3]—viz., violation of conservation of energy—does not apply in dual space-time.

6.6 Experimental test of mind-brain dualism

Now it is one thing to *say* that perception and will operate as described above, and another to show that it is so. Can this be done? The answer is that indeed it can, and it turns out to be perfectly straightforward and easy to perform.

6.6.1 The objective here is to demonstrate empirically the reality of perception and will in dual space-time. There is no need for external observers or instrumentation. Instead, the subject, a conscious being, is asked to observe visually her own willed action, such as a flick of the wrist. She is to estimate the time interval between her decision to act and her visual perception of that act. That interval can then be compared with the one expected for the same subject living (hypothetically) in ordinary space-time rather than dual space-time.

6.6.2 The basic logic flow of the test is shown in **Fig. 6.5(a)**. It is formed by uniting the will diagram of **Fig. 6.4** and the perception diagram of **Fig. 6.3**.

6.6.3 The process begins, as in **Fig. 6.4**, in the cortex dual with the decision to act. The subject holds this moment in memory as her moment of decision. There is at once projected into the *future* a visualized motor objective, ultimately to become a realized motor objective—the flick of the wrist—as depicted in **Fig. 6.4**. Note that both the visualized and realized motor objective occur at time zero in both **Figs. 6.4** and **6.5(a)**.

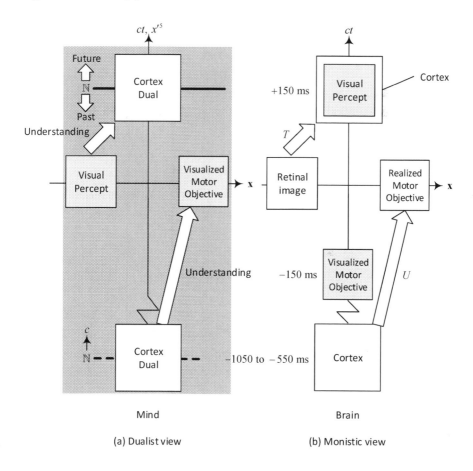

Mind   Brain

(a) Dualist view   (b) Monistic view

Fig. 6.5 (a) Logic flow when the subject observes the result of her own willed action in dual space-time. **(b)** Hypothetical logic flow when 4-D space-time is substituted for dual space-time. In this case, according to conventional neuroscience, the subject's motor objective arises not by will but unconsciously.

6.6.4 The perception process begins, as in **Fig. 6.3**, with the subject's willed hand motion—the realized motor objective—imaged onto her retina. This imaging step takes essentially no time at all (on the order of a nanosecond) owing to the speed of light. Perception, however, has not yet occurred. The signal generated at the retina must first travel to the visual cortex and main cortex, where it will be understood. Visual perception then takes place in the *past*, at time zero in both **Figs. 6.3** and **6.5(a)**.

6.6.5 What the subject understands at the moment of decision to act is her visualized motor objective; and what she understands at the moment of perception is the visual percept of her willed hand motion. As we can see from **Fig. 6.5(a)**, both the visualized motor objective and visual percept occur simultaneously at time zero. The temporal interval between them is zero. This prediction is easily confirmed. Decide to flick your wrist at the count of three. You will find that the visual image of your willed hand motion coincides precisely with the moment of your decision to act, with no delay whatsoever, *thereby corroborating our account of mind-brain dualism.*

6.7 Mind-brain monism: A thought experiment

Now suppose we could perform this same test in ordinary, four-dimensional space-time. This is the geometric setting assumed in scientific naturalism. What would the scientific naturalist predict for the interval between the subject's decision to act and her observation of that act?

6.7.1 The basic logic flow of this hypothetical test is shown in **Fig. 6.5(b)**. Because frame K_D is not involved, the diagram is formed by uniting the Brain portions *only* of the Will diagram of **Fig. 6.4** and Perception diagram of **Fig. 6.3**.

6.7.2 However, one additional piece of information is needed. In a now famous experiment led by Benjamin Libet,[4] measurement of electrical brain activity called the *readiness potential*[5] showed that an action performed that the subject *thinks* is voluntary allegedly begins *unconsciously*, roughly 900 to 400 milliseconds before the moment she estimates was the moment of her decision to act. That estimated moment turned out to precede the act itself by a mere 150 milliseconds. *On the basis of this experiment, the neuroscientific community has largely concluded that free will is an illusion.*[6] The subject's estimated 150 millisecond interval, not coincidentally, happens also to be the time it takes for the electrochemical signal from the retina to reach the visual cortex and lateral prefrontal cortex for processing and understanding.[7] In **Fig. 6.5(b)** the subject's visualized motor objective is shown preceding the realized motor objective by precisely this value.

6.7.2 The experiment begins (according to naturalistic neuroscience) unconsciously, resulting in, by means of the same operation U shown in **Fig. 6.4,** the realized motor objective—a flex of the wrist, for example. This realized objective is then imaged, essentially instantaneously owing to the speed of light, onto the subject's retina. Finally, this image, by means of the same operation T shown in **Fig. 6.4**, is projected into the visual cortex and lateral prefrontal cortex for processing and understanding.

6.7.3 Now this latter step, as indicated in the diagram, takes 150 milliseconds to complete. Meanwhile, according to Libet, and as shown in the diagram, the subject's reported decision to act precedes the realized act by another 150 milliseconds. Therefore, conventional neuroscience predicts the interval experienced by the subject between her decision to act and her visual perception of it would be $150 + 150 = 300$ milliseconds. Such an interval corresponds to a metronome setting of 200 beats/minute, and would be easily discerned if it existed. But we have seen above that in such an experiment, when actually performed, the interval experienced is precisely zero. *Thus biological naturalism, mind-brain monism, and the notion that free-will is an illusion, are all falsified.* All of which illustrates, one might add, the danger of attempting to derive first-person experience from third-person measurements, and more particularly without knowledge of the dualistic structure of space-time.

6.8 Transcendent origin of conscious experience

This has been a lot of work to prove what we already know perfectly well: that we are fully capable of making conscious decisions, that free-will is no illusion, and more generally, that mind is no mere outcropping of the material brain. We are not robots. The comparison between the now-corroborated conscious being of **Fig. 6.1** and the robot of **Fig. 6.2** makes that clear.

So where does this remarkable dual mind-brain structure come from? How does it originate? Why in fact should we be in possession of it? The honest answer is that we don't know exactly. What we *do* know is that it could not have arisen directly or by evolution out of primordial soup in four space-time dimensions. For that would amount to the natural equivalent of building a conscious robot, which the cross-hatched barrier of **Fig. 6.2** prevents us from doing. And so, while we have some idea of what consciousness can do—perception, will, and understanding—just how machines like us came to be endowed with it remains a mystery.

We do, however, have a clue. For the conscious being is a self-referencing machine, and so can be depicted in communication-theoretic form, just as we have done for the physical world in **Fig. 2.1** and for God in **Figs. 3.2** and **5.1(a)**. This depiction, adapted from **Fig. 6.1**, is presented in **Fig. 6.6(a)**, where the shaded right-going arrow refers to perception and the shaded left-going arrow to the will. The similarity between the structures of conscious experience and of God [**Fig. 5.1(a)**] is apparent, the one difference being that conscious experience is bi-directional. In fact the similarity can be made even closer by taking into account these words of Jesus as reported by Saint John (John 14:6):[8] "I am the truth and the life. No one comes to the Father except through me." And more directly in the words of Peter speaking of Jesus to the Sanhedrin (Acts 4:12):[9] "There is no salvation in anyone else, for there is no other name in the whole world given to men by which we are to be saved." Thus we may add to **Fig. 5.1(a)** left-going arrows representing *salvation*, yielding the bi-directional structure of God depicted in **Fig. 6.6(b)**.

Comparing the two side-by-side depictions in **Fig. 6.6** we see that cortical Understanding is to conscious experience as the Holy Spirit is to the triune God: an intercessor linking object and image. The functional congruence between the conscious Self and God is unlikely

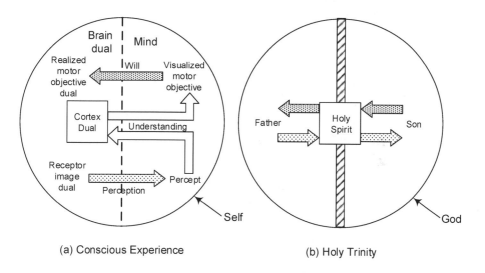

(a) Conscious Experience   (b) Holy Trinity

Fig. 6.6 (a) The Self's three-in-one structure of conscious experience, a bidirectional structure analogous to the unidirectional structure of the triune God of **Fig. 5.1(a)**, and even more closely analogous to the bidirectional structure of companion figure **(b)**. In **(b)** the right going arrows have the same significance as those in **Fig. 5.1(a)**; the left-going arrows signify *salvation* through the Son to the Father, as warranted in John 14:6 and Acts 4:12.

to be accidental. For as neither the percept nor motor objective are made of matter, and as both arise in the context of the (immaterial) Law of Laws Eq. (3.1), their existence—as well that of the Self experiencing them—may be taken as further evidence of a transcendent ordering principle, viz., the triune God. In that light, it appears literally the case that man is made in God's image and likeness.

Notes and references

[1] John T. Winthrop, *The Principle of True Representation: Mind, Matter and Geometry in a Self-Consistent Universe* (www.toplinkpublishing.com, 2019), 461-516.

[2] Winthrop, 467.

[3] Daniel C. Dennett, *Consciousness Explained* (New York: Back Bay Books, Little, Brown and Company, 1991), 35.

[4] B. Libet, C. A. Gleason, E. W. Wright and D. K. Pearl, "Time of conscious intention to act in relation to onset of cerebral activities (readiness-potential); the unconscious initiation of a freely voluntary act," *Brain* 106 (1983): 623-642; Benjamin Libet, "Do We Have Free Will?" in *The Volitional Brain*, Benjamin Libet, Anthony Freeman and Keith Sutherland, eds. (Thorverton, UK: Imprint Academic, 1999), 47-57.

[5] The readiness potential (RP) was discovered by H. H. Kornhuber and L. Deeke, "Hirnpotential ändrugen bei Willkürbewe und passive Bevegungen des Nenschen: Bereitschaftpotential und reafferente potentiale," Pflügers Archiv 284 (1965): 1-17. The RP is measurable by electroencephalogram (EEG) scans at the top of the head.

[6] For contemporary and historical arguments in support of this alleged illusion, see Daniel M. Wegner, *The Illusion of Conscious Will* (Cambridge, MA: The MIT Press, 2002); for counterarguments, see Julian Baggini, *Freedom Regained: The Possibility of Free Will* (Chicago: The University of Chicago Press, 2015).

[7] S. Thorpe, D. Fize and C. Marlot, "Speed of processing in the human visual system," *Nature* 381 (June 6, 1996): 520-522.

[8] *The New American Bible* (Catholic Book Publishing Co., New York, 1970). Hereafter referred to as *TNAB*.

[9] *TNAB*

Chapter 7

Natural moral law

This book argues from systems theory not only that God exists but that we are indeed made in his image and likeness. Thus, because among God's attributes is moral perfection, we too should possess an intrinsic—or "natural"—moral sense. Our purpose in this chapter is to show, in terms of the structure of existence set forth earlier in the book, precisely how that law is established in the human psyche.

7.1 What is natural law?

Laws are obligatory bindings of one form or another. Thus in the social sphere, one is obliged by tax law to turn over a portion of one's income to governing authority. In economics, markets obey the law of supply and demand. In mathematics, the angles and sides of a triangle obey the law of sines. And in physics, massive bodies obey Newton's law of gravitation.

The law we are going to consider here is of a different kind than those just mentioned. I refer in particular to *revealed* law, a precept guiding our moral and ethical treatment of one another known as *natural moral law*, or simply *natural law*.

Scripturally natural law is handed down to us in two forms, old and new. The *old* form is the Decalogue, or Ten Commandments, revealed in two books of the Old Testament: *Exodus* 20:1-17 and *Deuteronomy* 5:6-22.[1] The *new* law came resoundingly from Jesus, who, when asked "Which is the first of all the commandments?", replied: (*Mark* 12:28-32)[2]

> "This is the first:
> 'Hear, O Israel! The Lord our God is Lord alone!
> Therefore you shall love the Lord your God
> with all your heart,

> with all your soul,
> with all your mind,
> and with all your strength.'
> This is the second,
> 'You shall love your neighbor as yourself.'[3]
> There is no other commandment greater than these."

And thus by implication the Golden Rule: "Treat others the way you would have them treat you."[4]

These same two commandments of Jesus appear in *Matthew* 22:37-39, to which Jesus adds in clear reference to the old law, "On these two commandments the whole law is based, and the prophets as well." In other words, along with the new laws Jesus acknowledges the authority of the old. In fact, earlier in *Matthew* 5:17 Jesus remarks, "Do not think that I came to destroy the Law or the Prophets. I did not come to destroy but to fulfill." The essential unity of the old and new laws is later reinforced by St. Paul in *Romans* 13:8-10:[5]

> He who loves his neighbor has fulfilled the law. The commandments, "You shall not commit adultery; you shall not murder; you shall not steal; you shall not covet," and any other commandment there may be are all summed up in this "You shall love your neighbor as yourself." Love never wrongs the neighbor, hence love is the fulfillment of the law.

7.2 Natural versus conventional law

I stressed above that natural law differs in kind from conventional forms of law. The difference between them is just this: While conventional laws are formulated by human beings observing and thinking about the world around them, the natural moral law arises secretly and unbidden within us, whether one acknowledges it not. As St. Paul puts it in *Romans* 2:14-15,[6]

> When Gentiles who do not have the law keep it as by instinct, these men although without the law serve as a law for themselves. They show that the demands of the law are written in their hearts.

Thus, according to St. Paul, the moral attitude is instinctive, not learned, though of course it can disregarded. And why is it of this form? Because, according to Catholic Church doctrine, and as demonstrated in the previous chapter, we are made in the image and likeness of God:[7]

> Man judges rightly that by his intellect he surpasses the material universe, for he shares in the light of the divine mind.
>
> In the depths of his conscience, man detects a law which he does not impose upon himself, but which holds him to obedience. Always summoning him to love good and avoid evil, the voice of conscience when necessary speaks to his heart; do this, shun that. For man has in his heart a law written by God; to obey it is the very dignity of man; according to it he will be judged.

Morality is, in other words, teleological in origin; its presence in us proceeds from the revelation that we are made in God's image and likeness, that we share in God's love of good and avoidance of evil. Note the inversion of the teleological argument discussed in **Chapter 1**. Scripture infers morality from God, not God's existence from morality. Note too that the analogy relates to first-person inner structure—that of God and mind—not the third-person external structure of conventional teleology.

7.3 God is Love

We shall now attempt to go beyond teleological argument and actually *derive* the presence in man of a transcendently given natural law of the form "You shall love your neighbor as yourself." The first step in this effort is to see how love fits into the structure of human consciousness. The second step is to show how love, once embedded in consciousness, works to the benefit of one's fellow creatures. The third and final step is to argue empirically for the law's transcendent origin.

7.3.1 Connecting love and consciousness is not difficult to do. It is a matter of noting the similarity of their structures, then uniting them.

(a) Consider first the structure of love. In his treatise *On the Trinity*, Book Nine, St. Augustine argues that love, like God, is Trinitarian in nature:[8]

> Well then, when I, who make this inquiry, love anything, there are three things concerned—myself, and that which I love, and love itself. For I do not love love, except I love a lover; for there is no love where nothing is loved. Therefore there are three things—he who loves, and that which is loved, and love.

And so, thanks to St. Augustine, we recognize in love three inseparable components: the lover, the beloved, and love itself.

(b) As for consciousness, in the previous chapter it was shown that consciousness, with its three functional components perception, will, and understanding, likewise parallels the triune structure of God; see **Fig. 6.6**.

(c) Now suppose that there exists no one other than oneself. Then the only love possible is that of oneself, a category of love presupposed in Jesus' second moral law. St. Augustine's three things in that case become: the loving self, the beloved self, and love itself. These three things run in parallel with the three functional components of the single being's consciousness:

Will ↔ The loving self
Percept ↔ The beloved self
Understanding ↔ Love itself

The structure of self-love in the conscious being, based on these correspondences, is depicted schematically in **Fig. 7.1(a)**. Two features stand out. First, self-love spans both mind and brain, without which dualist structure there can be no conscious experience at all, much less self-love. Second, within that structure, self-love circulates between mind and brain, as befits the self-knowing, self-aware conscious being. Specifically, in analogy with *perception*, a cortical representation of the beloved self proceeds to the mind, forming there an implicit image or awareness of the beloved self. This implicit image is then, by way of

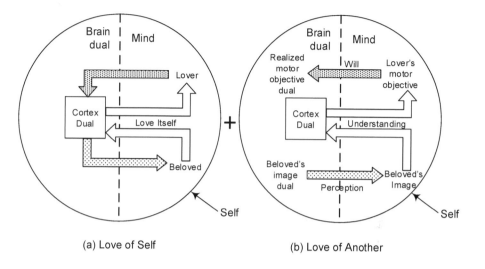

(a) Love of Self   (b) Love of Another

Fig. 7.1 (a) Illustrating the self-referencing structure of self-love. **(b)** Illustrating the structure of one's love for another. The two figures together, joined by the "plus sign" illustrates the structure of Jesus' second law.

love itself, *understood* as such by the cortical mechanism giving rise to it, which mechanism then returns to the mind an implicit image of the one who loves—the lover himself. Finally, in analogy with *will*, the lover's motivation to love oneself returns to the cortex, reinforcing there the representation of the beloved self, whence the cycle begins again, *ad infinitum.*

7.3.2 This cyclic structure of self-love remains a constant presence in the core of the conscious being, providing a basis and model for that being's behavior toward others. When one loves oneself, it becomes possible—by extension—to love others. From a systems-theory point of view, such an act appears no different from other interactions with one's environment. It can be diagrammed as in **Fig. 7.1(b)**, wherein the "Beloved's image" and "Lover's motor objective" become, respectively, the "Percept" and "Visualized motor objective" of **Fig. 6.6(a),** the latter figure illustrating conscious experience in general. The act of love toward others is nevertheless unique in being motivated by an underlying principle of self-love; hence the "plus sign" shown between depictions **(a)** and **(b)** of **Fig. 7.1**. This arithmetic symbol corresponds to the word "as" in Jesus' second law. **Figure 7.1**, with plus sign included, embraces this second law in its entirety.

7.3.3 And so, on the present theory, behavior toward others proceeds from an underlying principle of self-love. Consequently, to understand where the law in its entirety comes from, one need only locate the ultimate origin of self-love. We strongly suspect that self-love, owing to the similarity of its structure to that of conscious experience, also derives from the three-fold structure of God. Nevertheless, another source for the presence of self-love in man is at least imaginable, namely, the biology of evolution. Let us explore this possibility.

Oddly enough, a clue suggesting an evolutionary origin of self-love is provided by St. Paul, who in the above passage from Romans refers to the law as one obeyed by *instinct*, even by non-believers. Now we know of another behavioral instinct, that of self-preservation, better known as the *survival instinct*. This is simply the desire of apparently all living beings, humans in particular, to avoid annihilation, to continue to exist. Suppose we ask where *that* instinct comes from, with a view to seeing its relationship, if any, to that of self-love.

According to evolutionary biology, the survival instinct relates to a given being's perceived ability to reproduce.[9] On this view a strong or weak sense of reproductive potential translates to a corresponding strong or weak desire to remain alive. But then the so-called survival instinct reduces to nothing more than a barometer of one's own sense of reproductive potential. We must then ask, If the sense of the need to reproduce is fundamental, then where does *that* sense come from? Implied is a backwards causal chain of explanation, perhaps infinite, one in any case having no obvious beginning. With this line of reasoning we find no plausible *biological* explanation for the most basic of inner drives, that of self-preservation.

Thus, in the absence of biological explanation, we are led to attribute the survival instinct to self-love. The intense universal desire to maintain one's own existence then becomes easy to understand. For one cannot love a non-living, non-existent self. But if the survival instinct cannot be explained biologically, then self-love, which precedes and underwrites the survival instinct, cannot be explained that way either. Its only plausible remaining place of origin, like that of the structure of conscious experience, is the Holy Trinity itself. *The instinct for self-love thus proves to be of transcendental origin,* as suspected at the beginning of this subsection. Of course that does not mean that the rule to love thy neighbor, which flows from self-love, will necessarily be followed. Just as the survival instinct may decline in the face of poor reproductive potential, man endowed with free will is more than capable of disobedience.[10]

The logic tree of **Fig. 17.2** summarizes our argument for the transcendent origin of the Golden Rule.

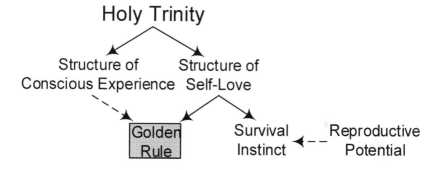

Fig. 7.2 Logic tree illustrating the Golden Rule's ultimate origin in the Holy Trinity. Conscious Experience and Self-Love are both structurally consistent with the three-fold structure of the Holy Trinity and accordingly are shown descending from that structure. Self-Love, structurally embedded in the human psyche, provides an inner model for behavior towards others. The Golden Rule, shown descending from the entwined structures of Self-Love and Conscious Experience, thus proves ultimately to be of transcendent origin—natural moral law. The dashed arrow from Conscious Experience indicates that, owing to free will, the natural moral law may not always be obeyed. The structure of Self-Love accounts also for the Survival Instinct. According to evolutionary biology, and as suggested by the dashed arrow, the strength of that instinct varies in accordance to one's sense of reproductive potential

Notes and references

[1] *The New American Bible* (Catholic Book Publishing Co., New York, 1970). Hereafter referred to as *TNAB*.

[2] *TNAB*

[3] Here by "neighbor" Jesus means *all* men, including enemies. The same law was set down nearly six centuries earlier in Leviticus 19:18 but referred there, not to all men, but to the treatment of one's "fellow countrymen."

[4] See Matthew 7:12 and Luke 6:31. Confucius (551-479 B. C.) expounded a negative expression of the Golden Rule: "Do not do to others what you would not desire yourself." See *The Sayings of Confucius*, James R. Ware, trans. (New York: Mentor, 1955), 76.

[5] *TNAB*

[6] *TNAB*

[7] *Gaudium et Spec,* 15, 16.

[8] St. Augustine, "On the Trinity," *Basic Writings of St. Augustine*, Volume 2, Whitney J. Oates, ed. (Grand Rapids: Baker Books, 1992), 790.

[9] R. M. Brown, E. Dahlen, C.Mills, J. Rick, A. Blarz, "Evaluation of an evolutionary model of self-preservation and self-destruction," *Suicide and Life-Threatening Behavior* 29, no.1 (Spring, 1999): 58-71;
https://www.ncbi.nlm.nih.gov/pubmed/10322621.

[10] In this connection see Alvin Plantinga, *God, Freedom, and Evil* (Grand Rapids, MI: Wm. B. Eerdmans Publishing Co., 1977), Ch. 4.

Chapter 8

Conclusion

If we submit everything to reason our religion will be left with nothing mysterious or supernatural.

    If we offend the principles of reason our religion will be absurd and ridiculous.

BLAISE PASCAL, Pensées, 173.

This book argues that to prove the existence of God, one must first prove, beyond a reasonable doubt, the existence of the external world. For if we cannot do that, then we shall have failed to show that God exists anywhere but in the mind. How, then, do we prove that the world is truly real and not a dream? Descartes convinced himself of his *own* existence when he realized that he was in a position to doubt it; that he could be, in other words, the object of his own thinking. We apply here a similar principle of self-reference to the problem of the external world: the Principle of True Representation. This principle, applied in a communication-theoretic context, unifies the worlds of appearance and reality, leading at once to a formal signature X of the existence of the external world. Signature X, an algebraic structure here denoted the Law of Laws, is corroborated empirically, demonstrating beyond a reasonable doubt the existence of the external world.

Next we show that God, if he exists, is marked by a signature of existence X of the same form as that marking the external world. But this signature of the world's existence, while empirically corroborated and thus perfectly real, is immaterial, meaning that the material world could not have invented and imposed it upon itself. It must, therefore, have been imposed upon the world by another agent entirely, namely by God, who by nature is immaterial, and whose signature of existence is the same as that of the world. Thus, because the world exists, so must God exist. This is the existential argument for the existence of God. It is also the title of this book.

God's signature X defines a system of three components, an input, an output, and a system operator acting on the input to yield the output. The system is self-representing because, owing to the PTR, the output is proportional to the input. Although defined in non-spiritual terms, this system-theoretic characterization of God nevertheless appears consistent with the triune God of Christianity; the Father as input, the Son as output, and the Holy Spirit acting with the Father to yield the Son.

In the epigraph to this brief concluding chapter, Pascal worries about the demystification of religion by overanalyzing it. The philosopher need not be concerned. For no amount of thinking can reveal in full the attributes of an invisible God. Nor can it resolve the mystery of why anything, including God, should exist at all. He is right, however, to encourage rational understanding of the object of faith. For according to the existential argument, God does exist, and if that is so, not only is faith warranted, but new light is thrown on the enduring questions of life and mind.

We have discovered that the three-in-one God defined by signature X lives, not in ordinary space-time, but in a frame of reference dual to that of the world of matter and energy. It is the very frame required to support conscious experience, the structure of which phenomenon closely resembles the triune structure of God. Thus man justifiably may be said to be made in God's image and likeness. All of which suggests, against all rational expectation, that God, as a principle of self-knowing, may dwell directly in conscious life and perhaps, on evolutionary grounds, in all life, conscious or not. A key consequence of this indwelling is natural moral law, whose presence in man we have shown to be directly attributable to God's three-in-one structure. On the evidence presented here, I suggest that science and religion, as against Stephen Jay Gould's argument for their separation,[1] not only overlap, but comprise a single discipline, one not yet named, but worthy of further exploration.

Reference

[1] Steven Jay Gould, *Rocks of Ages: Science and Religion in the Fullness of Life* (New York: The Ballantine Publishing Group, 1999), Ch. 2.

Index

Index

G

God
    and conscious experience, 45
    and love
        origin of natural moral law, 61
    and scientific method, 35
    and time, 36
    classic arguments
        cosmological, 8
        ontological, 7
        teleological, 9
    existence of, ix, 3, 5, 6, 16, 42, 67
    existential argument, 12, 25, 33, 68
        comparison to classic arguments, 35
    First Cause, 9
    geometric setting for, 29
    image of, 29, 41
    indwelling, 68
    logical structure of, ix
    neural correlate of, 6
    problem of, 25
    self-knowing, 68
    signature of, 30, 41
    the Father, 41
    the Holy Spirit, 41
    the Son, 41
    triune, 3, 41, 42, 68
Golden Rule, 60
Gospel, 41
Gould, Stephen Jay, 68
gravitational force, 21
graviton, 21

H

Hegel, Georg Wlhelm Friedrich, 36
Hofstader, Douglas, 19
Holy Spirit
    divine intercessor, 41, 44
    Eastern Orthodox, 44
    Paraclete, 44
    Western Church, 44
Holy Trinity
    depicted in the Athanasian Creed, 43

depicted in the existential argument, 43

I

identity theory, 6
intelligent design, 10

J

Jesus
    as Son of God the Father, 41
    as Word, 41
Judas, 44

K

Kant, Immanuel, 5

L

law
    conventional, 59
    Decalogue, 59
    Golden Rule, 60
    natural moral, 68
        origin
            teleological, 61
            transcendent, 61
        vs. conventional law, 60
    natural noral, 59
    revealed, 59
Law of Laws, 18, 19, 23, 33, 67
    reality of, 36
Laws of Physics, 4
Libet, Benjamin, 57
love, 61
    origin of natural moral law, 65
    Trinitarian nature of, 62

M

mathematics, in the physical sciences, 22
Meditations, Descarte's, 15
metaphysics, ix, x, 19
mind

72

Printed in the United States
By Bookmasters